Revelation

The New Jerusalem

(Chapters 13-22)

Group Directory

Pass this Directory around and have your Group Members
fill in their names and phone numbers

Name   **Phone**

_____   _____

_____   _____

_____   _____

_____   _____

_____   _____

_____   _____

_____   _____

_____   _____

_____   _____

_____   _____

_____   _____

_____   _____

Revelation

EDITING AND PRODUCTION TEAM:

James F. Couch, Jr., Lyman Coleman, Sharon Penington, Cathy Tardif,
Christopher Werner, Matthew Lockhart, Erika Tiepel, Richard Peace,
Andrew Sloan, Mike Shepherd, Gregory C. Benoit,
Margaret Harris, Katharine Harris, Scott Lee

NASHVILLE, TENNESSEE

Published by Serendipity House Publishers

Nashville, Tennessee

International Standard Book Number: 1-57494-328-6

ACKNOWLEDGMENTS

Scripture quotations are taken from the Holman Christian Standard Bible,
© Copyright 2000 by Holman Bible Publishers. Used by permission.

03 04 05 06 07 08 / 10 9 8 7 6 5 4 3 2

Nashville, Tennessee

1-800-525-9563

www.serendipityhouse.com

Table of Contents

Core Values

Community: The purpose of this curriculum is to build community within the body of believers around Jesus Christ.

Group Process: To build community, the curriculum must be designed to take a group through a step-by-step process of sharing your story with one another.

Interactive Bible Study: To share your "story," the approach to Scripture in the curriculum needs to be open-ended and right brain—to "level the playing field" and encourage everyone to share.

Developmental Stages: To provide a healthy program throughout the four stages of the life cycle of a group, the curriculum needs to offer courses on three levels of commitment: (1) Beginner Level—low-level entry, high structure, to level the playing field; (2) Growth Level—deeper Bible study, flexible structure, to encourage group accountability; (3) Discipleship Level—in-depth Bible study, open structure, to move the group into high gear.

Target Audiences: To build community throughout the culture of the church, the curriculum needs to be flexible, adaptable and transferable into the structure of the average church.

Mission: To expand the Kingdom of God one person at a time by filling the "empty chair." (We add an extra chair to each group session to remind us of our mission.)

Introduction

Each healthy small group will move through various stages as it matures.

Multiply Stage: The group begins the multiplication process. Members pray about their involvement in new groups. The "new" groups begin the life cycle again with the Birth Stage.

Birth Stage: This is the time in which group members form relationships and begin to develop community. The group will spend more time in ice-breaker exercises, relational Bible study and covenant building.

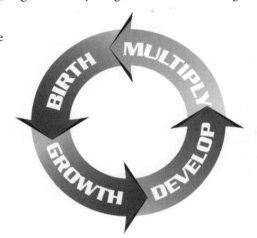

Develop Stage: The inductive Bible study deepens while the group members discover and develop gifts and skills. The group explores ways to invite their neighbors and coworkers to group meetings.

Growth Stage: Here the group begins to care for one another as it learns to apply what they learn through Bible study, worship and prayer.

Subgrouping: If you have nine or more people at a meeting, Serendipity recommends you divide into subgroups of 3–6 for the Bible study. Ask one person to be the leader of each subgroup and to follow the directions for the Bible study. After 30 minutes, the Group Leader will call "time" and ask all subgroups to come together for the Caring Time.

Each group meeting should include all parts of the "three-part agenda."

 Ice-Breaker: Fun, history-giving questions are designed to warm the group and to build understanding about the other group members. You can choose to use all of the Ice-Breaker questions, especially if there is a new group member that will need help in feeling comfortable with the group.

 Bible Study: The heart of each meeting is the reading and examination of the Bible. The questions are open, discover questions that lead to further inquiry. Reference notes are provided to give everyone a "level playing field." The emphasis is on understanding what the Bible says and applying the truth to real life. The questions for each session build. There is always at least one "going deeper" question provided. You should always leave time for the last of the "questions for interaction." Should you choose, you can use the optional "going deeper" question to satisfy the desire for the challenging questions in groups that have been together for a while.

 Caring Time: All study should point us to actions. Each session ends with prayer and direction in caring for the needs of the group members. You can choose between several questions. You should always pray for the "empty chair." Who do you know that could fill that void in your group?

Sharing Your Story: These sessions are designed for members to share a little of their personal lives each time. Through a number of special techniques, each member is encouraged to move from low risk, less personal sharing to higher risk responses. This helps develop the sense of community and facilitates caregiving.

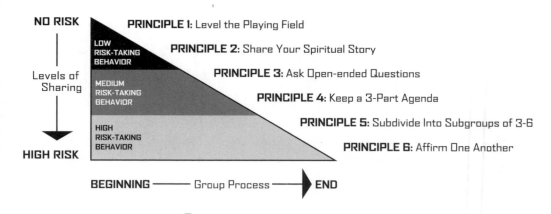

NO RISK

LOW RISK-TAKING BEHAVIOR

Levels of Sharing

MEDIUM RISK-TAKING BEHAVIOR

HIGH RISK-TAKING BEHAVIOR

HIGH RISK

PRINCIPLE 1: Level the Playing Field

PRINCIPLE 2: Share Your Spiritual Story

PRINCIPLE 3: Ask Open-ended Questions

PRINCIPLE 4: Keep a 3-Part Agenda

PRINCIPLE 5: Subdivide Into Subgroups of 3-6

PRINCIPLE 6: Affirm One Another

BEGINNING —— Group Process —➤ END

Group Covenant: A group covenant is a "contract" that spells out your expectations and the ground rules for your group. It's very important that your group discuss these issues—preferably as part of the first session.

Ground Rules:

- Priority: While you are in the group, you give the group meeting priority.

- Participation: Everyone participates and no one dominates.

- Respect: Everyone is given the right to their own opinion and all questions are encouraged and respected.

- Confidentiality: Anything that is said in the meeting is never repeated outside the meeting.

- Empty Chair: The group stays open to new people at every meeting.

- Support: Permission is given to call upon each other in time of need—even in the middle of the night.

- Advice Giving: Unsolicited advice is not allowed.

- Mission: We agree to do everything in our power to start a new group as our mission.

Issues:

- The time and place this group is going to meet is _____.

- Refreshments are _____ responsibility.

- Child care is _____ responsibility.

SESSION 1
The Two Beasts
REVELATION 13:1–18

Welcome

Welcome to this study of the last half of the book of Revelation. In the last session of Book 1, we watched as Satan was cast down from heaven, and discovered the real source of his rage against mankind: he is angry with God. This week we will make the unpleasant acquaintance of two of Satan's servants, and we will watch as they perform their blasphemies against the kingdom of God.

Ice-Breaker   15 Min.
CONNECT WITH YOUR GROUP

LEADER

Be sure to read the introductory material in the front of this book prior to the first session. To help your group members get acquainted, have each person introduce him or herself and then take turns answering one or two of the Ice-Breaker questions.

Some people seem to have a real gift of charisma, and are able to charm their way into anyone's heart. Some people seem downright scary. But some of us have looked at the most frightening face of all—the face of Death. Take a few minutes to get to know one another with the following questions.

1. What is your favorite classic monster movie?

   ○ *Creature from the Black Lagoon.*
   ○ *Godzilla.*
   ○ *King Kong.*
   ○ Other _____.

2. Who have been the most charismatic leaders in your lifetime? What made those people such compelling leaders?

3. Is there someone you know who has had a near-death experience? What brought that person back to life?

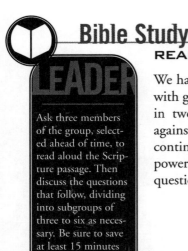

Bible Study

READ SCRIPTURE AND DISCUSS

LEADER

Ask three members of the group, selected ahead of time, to read aloud the Scripture passage. Then discuss the questions that follow, dividing into subgroups of three to six as necessary. Be sure to save at least 15 minutes for the Caring Time.

We have seen Satan, our ancient enemy, fall from heaven and land with great rage on earth. Today we will watch in horror as he brings in two henchmen to help with his wicked work, blaspheming against the kingdom of God. But we will not despair, for John will continue to assure us that God has all things completely under his power. Read the following passage from Revelation, then discuss the questions that follow.

The Two Beasts

Reader One:

13 And I saw a beast coming up out of the sea. He had 10 horns and seven heads. On his horns were 10 diadems, and on his heads were blasphemous names. ²The beast I saw was like a leopard, his feet were like a bear's, and his mouth was like a lion's mouth. The dragon gave him his power, his throne, and great authority. ³One of his heads appeared to be fatally wounded, but his fatal wound was healed. The whole earth was amazed and followed the beast. ⁴They worshiped the dragon because he gave authority to the beast. And they worshiped the beast, saying, "Who is like the beast? Who is able to wage war against him?"

Reader Two:

⁵A mouth was given to him to speak boasts and blasphemies. He was also given authority to act for 42 months. ⁶He began to speak blasphemies against God: to blaspheme His name and His dwelling—those who dwell in heaven. ⁷And he was permitted to wage war against the saints and to conquer them. He was also given authority over every tribe, people, language, and nation. ⁸All those who live on the earth will worship him, everyone whose name was not written from the foundation of the world in the book of life of the Lamb who was slaughtered.

Reader Three:

⁹If anyone has an ear, he should listen:
¹⁰If anyone is destined for captivity,
    into captivity he goes.
    If anyone is to be killed with a sword,
    with a sword he will be killed.
    Here is the endurance and the faith of the saints.

Reader One:

¹¹Then I saw another beast coming up out of the earth; he had two horns like a lamb, but he sounded like a dragon. ¹²He exercises all the authority of the first beast on his behalf and compels the earth and those who live on it to worship the first beast,

whose fatal wound was healed. ¹³He also performs great signs, even causing fire to come down from heaven to earth before people. ¹⁴He deceives those who live on the earth because of the signs that he is permitted to perform on behalf of the beast, telling those who live on the earth to make an image of the beast who had the sword wound yet lived. ¹⁵He was permitted to give a spirit to the image of the beast, so that the image of the beast could both speak and cause whoever would not worship the image of the beast to be killed. ¹⁶And he requires everyone—small and great, rich and poor, free and slave—to be given a mark on his right hand or on his forehead, ¹⁷so that no one can buy or sell unless he has the mark: the beast's name or the number of his name.

Reader Two: ¹⁸Here is wisdom: The one who has understanding must calculate the number of the beast, because it is the number of a man. His number is 666.

Revelation 13:1–18

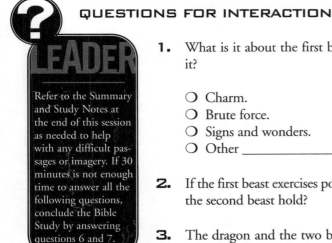

QUESTIONS FOR INTERACTION

Refer to the Summary and Study Notes at the end of this session as needed to help with any difficult passages or imagery. If 30 minutes is not enough time to answer all the following questions, conclude the Bible Study by answering questions 6 and 7.

1. What is it about the first beast that causes the world to worship it?

   ○ Charm.
   ○ Brute force.
   ○ Signs and wonders.
   ○ Other _____.

2. If the first beast exercises political power, what type of power does the second beast hold?

3. The dragon and the two beasts form a sort of unholy trinity. In what other ways do these evil entities imitate and mock the power of God?

4. The second beast had "two horns like a lamb, but he sounded like a dragon." Why does he appear like a lamb? Why does he speak like a dragon?

5. Who are some real people or entities down through history who have appeared like a lamb but spoken like a dragon?

6. Who are some of the beasts or idols in your life that test your allegiance to Christ?

7. How do you know if your name is written in the "book of life" (v. 8)?

GOING DEEPER:

If your group has time and/or wants a challenge, go on to this question.

8. Note the frequent use of the word "permitted" in this passage. All power, authority, and events come from God. Find the ways in which John subtly stresses this fact here.

Caring Time   15 Min.

APPLY THE LESSON AND PRAY FOR ONE ANOTHER

LEADER

Take some extra time in this first session to go over the introductory material at the front of this book. At the close, pass around your books and have everyone sign the Group Directory in the front of this book.

The things of eternity are not to be taken lightly, especially since we only have one lifetime in which to prepare for it. The first and most important step is to ensure that our names are written in the Lamb's book of life.

1. Is your name written in the book of life?

2. Are you struggling at present with something or someone who competes with your allegiance to Christ? How can this group help to strengthen your faithfulness to God?

3. Take some extra time in prayer, focusing on the fact that God has absolute control over all things. Pray especially for those in the group who are suffering or struggling with "divided allegiance."

Next Week

This week, we met two dreadful beings who assist Satan in his business of blaspheming God. However, we were comforted with the knowledge that anyone who belongs to Jesus can never be harmed by these ferocious foes. In the coming week, consider if there are any things in your own life which may be causing you to have a divided allegiance. Next week we will witness further judgments against humanity, as God's cup of wrath begins to be poured out.

SUMMARY: John recounts the works of the two beasts: the one from the sea (13:1b–10) and the one from the earth (13:11–18). The second beast arises who is a servant to the first beast. His purpose is to cause people to worship the first beast. He is probably meant to represent organized religion. He is later called the false prophet (16:13; 19:20; 20:10). With the coming of this beast, the evil trinity is complete. Satan, the Antichrist and the false prophet oppose God the Father, the Son and the Holy Spirit.

13:1 *a beast.* This is the Antichrist. The idea of the Antichrist is found throughout the Bible. The first mention is in Daniel 7, where he makes war against God's people. Jesus spoke of "the abomination that causes desolation" who will persecute God's people (Mark 13:14). Paul called this figure "the man of lawlessness" because he will oppose God (2 Thess. 2:3–4). He is inspired by Satan and he will seek to deceive people (2 Thess. 2:9–10). *out of the sea.* The sea was often considered to be a place of evil. *10 horns and seven heads.* Like the dragon, the beast has multiple heads and horns. There is a difference, however. The dragon has seven crowns on his heads, while the beast has 10 crowns on his horns. These 10 crowns represent 10 kings (17:12). *on his heads were blasphemous names.* The beast has taken to himself divine names. In verse 4 he is worshiped. This accords with Paul's description of the man of lawlessness (2 Thess. 2:4).

13:2 This beast has all the attributes of the four beasts in Daniel 7. He is the embodiment of evil, in that his power is derived from Satan. In Daniel, these beasts represent four kingdoms which were hostile to God.

13:3 The beast was slain by the sword but later revived (v. 14). This parallels the fate of the Lamb who was slain (5:6).

13:4 *they worshiped the beast.* Arrayed against God and the Messiah are the dragon (Satan) and beast (the Antichrist) in a kind of supernatural symmetry, continuing the parallelism begun in verse 3. They set themselves up as counterfeit deities. The aim of the beast is not just political power as the crowns suggest, but religious power. He seeks to gain the allegiance of the people and so subvert them from worship of the true God.

13:5 Thus the beast speaks as if he were God, in accord with Daniel 7:8,20,25. *42 months.* Once again the same number appears. This is the length of time of the great persecution.

13:6 *blaspheme.* Not only does the beast claim to possess that which belongs to God alone (Acts 12:20–25) he goes further and actually curses and reviles God. This is an overt act of mocking the Almighty.

13:7 The beast turns his wrath against the people of God. This is a time of great persecution. This verse does not mean that the beast succeeded in turning the saints from allegiance to God to allegiance to himself; only that he was able to kill them. However, as it turns out, these martyrs have, in fact, won a great victory (15:2). *permitted.* The beast was allowed for this period of time to control the world.

13:8 All are required to worship the beast. Those who belong to the Lamb will die as martyrs because of their refusal to worship. *the book of life.* The registry of all who have been saved by faith in the crucified Lamb.

13:10 *the endurance and the faith.* Retribution will come, but not immediately. They must wait for that day.

13:11 *two horns like a lamb.* The second beast is a parody of Christ: a beast pretending to be a lamb.

sounded like a dragon. His voice gave away his true identity (Matt. 7:15–16).

13:14 *permitted.* In 13:5–7, when speaking about the first beast, the passive "is permitted" is used four times in the Greek text, emphasizing that the first beast was a front for Satan; so too here the point is made that this second beast has no independent power. It also is controlled by Satan; ultimately, his "permission"comes only from God. *an image of the beast.* He had a statue made of the first beast and used his power to make it speak. There were stories in the ancient world about statues that could speak. The intention behind this pseudomiracle is to mimic the power of God to bring life.

13:15 *cause ... to be killed.* It is the statute that commands the death of those who will not worship it, in this battle between God and Satan.

13:16 Satan continues to mimic God and his ways. Here he causes people to be sealed with the name of the beast, just as God's people were sealed with God's mark in 7:3. Now there are people sealed for God and those sealed for Satan. *mark.* Brands were put on animals. Some slaves were similarly marked with the name of their owner; certain religious devotees were tattooed. This term also referred to the imperial seal that was used on official documents and on coins.

13:18 *666.* Many attempts have been made to translate this number into a name. None really succeed, since all such translation is, in the end, guesswork. Some suggest that this is a symbol not a cryptogram, and that since 7 is the perfect number, each number in the mark falls short of such perfection. Satan and his kin try to mimic God but fall short.

SESSION 2
The Lamb and the Harvest
REVELATION 14:1–20

🌎 Last Week

Last week, we met the beast and his profane associate, the second beast. We saw them perform their blasphemies against God, but were comforted with the knowledge that God's people cannot be harmed for more than a "short time." This week we will learn more about what it means to be "sealed" with God's name, and we will watch the Lord reap the harvest of mankind's wickedness.

☕ Ice-Breaker   15 Min.
CONNECT WITH YOUR GROUP

LEADER

Begin the session with a word of prayer. Have your group members take turns sharing their responses to one, two or all three of the Ice-Breaker questions. Be sure that everyone gets a chance to participate.

Our backgrounds and experiences are all unique, each of us living life in ways that give us different perspectives on what we see. Some grow up on farms, some in the city; some love sweets, some love fruits and vegetables. But all of us can share an understanding of God's word. Take a few minutes to get to know one another with the following questions.

1. What is your favorite grape treat?

   ○ Wine.
   ○ Grape juice.
   ○ Grape jelly.
   ○ Plain grapes.
   ○ Other _____.

2. Have you ever had a desire to get a tattoo? What is it about tattoos that are so attractive to young people?

3. What farm tools have you used?

READ SCRIPTURE AND DISCUSS

LEADER

Have three group members, whom you have selected beforehand, read the following passage from Revelation. Then divide into subgroups of three to six and discuss the Questions for Interaction.

We meet again the 144,000 gathered at the throne of God, and learn more about who they are. As always, however, our focus is not on those gathered around the throne but on the one seated there. We will learn about God's tremendous grace, and also about his righteous wrath. Read the following passage from Revelation, then discuss the questions that follow.

The Lamb and the Harvest

Reader One: 14 Then I looked, and there on Mount Zion stood the Lamb, and with Him were 144,000 who had His name and His Father's name written on their foreheads. ²I heard a sound from heaven like the sound of cascading waters and like the rumbling of loud thunder. The sound I heard was also like harpists playing on their harps. ³They sang a new song before the throne and before the four living creatures and the elders, but no one could learn the song except the 144,000 who had been redeemed from the earth. ⁴These are the ones not defiled with women, for they have kept their virginity. These are the ones who follow the Lamb wherever He goes. They were redeemed from the human race as the firstfruits for God and the Lamb. ⁵No lie was found in their mouths; they are blameless.

Reader Two: ⁶Then I saw another angel flying in mid-heaven, having the eternal gospel to announce to the inhabitants of the earth—to every nation, tribe, language, and people. ⁷He spoke with a loud voice: "Fear God and give Him glory, because the hour of His judgment has come. Worship the Maker of heaven and earth, the sea and springs of water."

⁸A second angel followed, saying: "It has fallen, Babylon the Great has fallen, who made all nations drink the wine of her sexual immorality, which brings wrath."

Reader Three: ⁹And a third angel followed them and spoke with a loud voice: "If anyone worships the beast and his image and receives a mark on his forehead or on his hand, ¹⁰he will also drink the wine of God's wrath, which is mixed full strength in the cup of His anger. He will be tormented with fire and sulfur in the sight of the holy angels and in the sight of the Lamb, ¹¹and the smoke of their torment will go up forever and ever. There is no rest day or night for those who worship the beast and his image, or anyone who receives the mark of his name. ¹²Here is the endurance of the saints, who keep the commandments of God and the faith in Jesus."

Reader One: ¹³Then I heard a voice from heaven saying, "Write: Blessed are the dead who die in the Lord from now on."

"Yes," says the Spirit, "let them rest from their labors, for their works follow them!"

¹⁴Then I looked, and there was a white cloud, and One like the Son of Man was seated on the cloud, with a gold crown on His head and a sharp sickle in His hand. ¹⁵Another angel came out of the sanctuary, crying out in a loud voice to the One who was seated on the cloud, "Use your sickle and reap, for the time to reap has come, since the harvest of the earth is ripe." ¹⁶So the One seated on the cloud swung His sickle over the earth, and the earth was harvested.

Reader Two: ¹⁷Then another angel who also had a sharp sickle came out of the sanctuary in heaven. ¹⁸Yet another angel, who had authority over fire, came from the altar, and he called with a loud voice to the one who had the sharp sickle, "Use your sharp sickle and gather the clusters of grapes from earth's vineyard, because its grapes have ripened." ¹⁹So the angel swung his sickle toward earth and gathered the grapes from earth's vineyard, and he threw them into the great winepress of God's wrath. ²⁰Then the press was trampled outside the city, and blood flowed out of the press up to the horses' bridles for about 180 miles.

Revelation 14:1–20

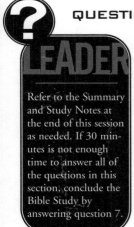

QUESTIONS FOR INTERACTION

Refer to the Summary and Study Notes at the end of this session as needed. If 30 minutes is not enough time to answer all of the questions in this section, conclude the Bible Study by answering question 7.

1. How are you like the 144,000 (vv. 1–5)? How are you unlike them?

2. What determines which people "drink the wine of God's wrath" and which will "rest from their labors?"

3. Babylon may be symbolic of man's attempts to create heaven on earth, to grow great while denying God. Here, Babylon has corrupted the whole world with its own evil practices. Are there such "Babylons" in the world today?

4. The sexual imagery in verse 4 may be symbolic of spiritual faithfulness to Christ. In what ways might the Christian church of today commit "adultery" with the world?

5. Consider the various metaphors used to describe God's wrath (such as strong wine, fire and sulfur, sharp sickles, etc.). What do these images convey about the wrath of God? Why is God so enraged about man's wickedness?

6. What cost have "the saints" in our time paid for following Christ? What costs have you paid?

7. How do you look upon death? What do you think it will be like? Are you prepared for it?

GOING DEEPER:

If your group has time and/or wants a challenge, go on to this question.

8. The followers of Christ have his name written on their foreheads; the worshipers of the beast have his name on their foreheads or right hands. What is the meaning of having a name on one's forehead? Why do the followers of Christ not have his name on their hands?

Caring Time 15 Min.

APPLY THE LESSON AND PRAY FOR ONE ANOTHER

LEADER

Bring the group members back together for the Caring Time. Begin by sharing responses to all three questions. Then share prayer requests and close in a group prayer. Those who do not feel comfortable praying out loud should not feel pressured to do so. As the leader, conclude the prayer time and be sure to pray for someone to fill the empty chair.

Walking with God brings us at times to paths that can be rough. It is not always easy to remain faithful to the one who has called us. We are called, however, to persevere, and groups such as this one can help to support those of us who may be finding the path to be hard.

1. Whose name is written on your forehead? Will you be standing with "the saints who keep the commandments of God and the faith in Jesus?"

2. Are you being faithful to Christ, or are you facing the temptations of the world to compromise?

3. Are you feeling weary—in need of God's rest—or spiritually energetic?

Next Week

This week we learned about the 144,000 who have been sealed with God's name on their foreheads, and we were encouraged to learn of the rest that is theirs forever. In the coming week, pray that the Lord will strengthen you to remain faithful and true to him, and encourage those who may be feeling weary. Next week, we will witness some more of God's wrath in the form of three plagues.

SUMMARY: In the interlude between the seven trumpets and the seven bowls, John continues to fill in the background out of which the final judgment will emerge. In this final section before the bowls of wrath are poured out, John describes a series of visions, each of which serves to assure his readers that the wicked will be judged and that the saints will be saved.

14:1 *Mount Zion.* In the vision of Joel, this is the place of deliverance for those who call upon the name of the Lord (Joel 2:32). This is the heavenly Zion, the Jerusalem that is above (Gal. 4:26; Heb. 12:22) since this whole scene takes place in a heavenly context.

14:4 This is the same 144,000 described in chapter 7:5–8. They are normally taken to be Jewish believers. Some take this verse to mean that the 144,000 are a special class of people who enjoy a special relationship with God and who are characterized by three things: abstinence from marriage (celibacy); following of the Lamb; and special consecration to God. Others consider that they are to be taken as the entire body of the redeemed. *not defiled with women.* It is true that both Jesus and Paul spoke approvingly of those who abstained from marriage (Matt. 19:12; 1 Cor. 7:1,32), but they also spoke approvingly of marriage (Matt. 19:4–6; Eph. 5:31–32). Furthermore, Israel was spoken of as a virgin in the Old Testament (2 Kin. 19:21; Jer. 18:13; Lam. 2:13; Amos 5:2), as was the church in the New Testament (2 Cor. 11:2). Therefore this phrase can be taken in a figurative sense, in which case the 144,000 would be the church (the spotless bride of Christ), who have not defiled themselves with the hostile world systems. *virginity.* This word can be translated "pure" or "chaste," and can refer to spiritual purity. John speaks of being aligned with the beast as "fornication" (14:8; 17:2; 18:3,9; 19:2). The concept of spiritual adultery is also found in the Old Testament (Jer. 3:6; Hos. 2:5). So this probably means that these people were the ones who kept themselves pure by not worshiping the beast. *follow the Lamb.* The 144,000 are not just characterized by what they did not do—they are also people who followed the teaching and

instructions of Jesus. They lived out his lifestyle (Mark 8:34).

14:6–13 The next vision has to do with three angels. The first proclaims the Gospel (vv. 6–7); the second announces the fall of Babylon (v. 8); and the third reveals the fate of those who follow the beast (vv. 9–11).

14:6 *to the inhabitants of the earth.* Again (e.g., 3:10; 6:10; 8:13) this refers to the people who do not worship and follow God. The angel is calling them to change their minds and ways and come to God. Yet again, on the eve of judgment, an appeal is made to those who stand outside God's kingdom.

14:7 *Maker of heaven and earth.* In the face of the powers of the beast, the angel asserts that it is God who made all of creation.

14:8 This is another announcement of what is yet to come (11:15; 12:10) as if it had just happened (17:1–18:24). *Babylon.* The original Babylon was a great city in Mesopotamia, renowned for its luxury and its corruption. It was also the traditional enemy of Israel. Here Babylon stands as the symbol of human society organized politically, economically, and religiously in defiance of God. *wine of her sexual immorality.* Babylon seduced the nations by her power, luxury, and corruption (17:2).

14:10 *fire and sulfur.* The lake of fire and brimstone is the symbol used in Revelation for the final place of Satan and his cohorts and followers (20:10,14–15). *in the sight of the holy angels/ Lamb.* See Mark 8:38 and Luke 12:9.

14:11 *their torment will go up forever and ever.* See Matthew 25:46.

14:12 This is not part of the angel's cry, but rather a comment following it. It was not easy to live in the realm of the beast, but faced with the implications of what it meant to be his follower in verses 9–11, the saint is encouraged to hang on and endure.

14:13 This idea is reinforced by the voice from heaven. Such endurance may well result in death, but the death of a saint is a death with a good outcome: eternal rest and reward for faithfulness. *from now on.* This is not to say that those who died before the Great Tribulation fail to be so blessed; it simply reminds those who are facing this terrible persecution that this is what awaits them. *rest from their labors.* This is not rest from ordinary work, but the cessation of the trials confronting those who seek to remain faithful to Jesus in the midst of a hostile kingdom.

14:14 *One like the Son of Man.* This title comes originally from Daniel 7:13–14; it was used extensively by Jesus as a title for himself (Mark 2:10). Here it identifies the Messiah who comes in judgment (Matt. 13:37–43; 25:31–46).

14:15 *out of the sanctuary.* The command to begin the judgment comes from God himself in his holy temple. *the harvest.* The image of harvest in the New Testament carries the idea both of gathering people into God's kingdom (Matt. 9:37–38) and of gathering the wicked for divine judgment (Matt. 13:30,40–42).

14:18 The idea of harvesting grapes is used elsewhere in the Bible as an image for judgment (Isa. 63:2–6; Joel 3:13).

14:20 The image shifts from wine to blood. The amount of blood is enormous. *up to the horses' bridles.* About four feet deep.

SESSION 3
Seven Last Plagues
REVELATION 15:1–8

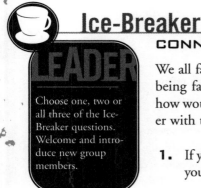

Last Week

Last time we learned about the 144,000 who have been sealed with the name of God on their foreheads, who "follow the Lamb wherever he goes." This week we will return yet again to the sanctuary, God's throne room, and will witness his great glory as his wrath is about to be poured out once more.

Ice-Breaker   15 Min.

CONNECT WITH YOUR GROUP

LEADER

Choose one, two or all three of the Ice-Breaker questions. Welcome and introduce new group members.

We all fantasize from time to time about winning great contests or being famous celebrities. Suppose that those dreams came true—how would you react? Take a few minutes to get to know one another with the following questions.

1. If you won a trophy with a big gold bowl at the top, what would you fill it with to celebrate?

   ○ Cherries.
   ○ Champagne.
   ○ Money.
   ○ Sweat and tears.
   ○ Other _____.

2. Have you ever won a great victory? What was it? How did you feel?

3. Is there a song or hymn that fills you with courage or that causes you to feel the grandeur of God's plan?

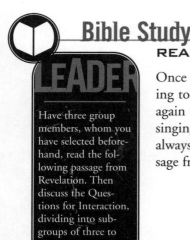

Bible Study   30 Min.

LEADER

Have three group members, whom you have selected beforehand, read the following passage from Revelation. Then discuss the Questions for Interaction, dividing into subgroups of three to six.

Once again, as we enter God's sanctuary, we see some angels preparing to pour forth the wrath of God upon the earth. We also meet again the redeemed, standing on a mysterious sea of glass and fire, singing the praises of the God who saved them. The focus here, as always, is on the majesty and glory of God. Read the following passage from Revelation, then discuss the questions that follow.

Seven Last Plagues

Reader One: 15 Then I saw another great and awe-inspiring sign in heaven: seven angels with the seven last plagues, for with them, God's wrath will be completed. ²I also saw something like a sea of glass mixed with fire, and those who had won the victory from the beast, his image, and the number of his name, were standing on the sea of glass with harps from God. ³They sang the song of God's servant Moses, and the song of the Lamb:

Reader Two: Great and awe-inspiring are Your works, Lord God, the Almighty;
righteous and true are Your ways, King of the Nations.
⁴Lord, who will not fear and glorify Your name?
Because You alone are holy,
because all the nations will come and worship before You,
because Your righteous acts have been revealed.

Reader Three: ⁵After this I looked, and the heavenly sanctuary—the tabernacle of testimony—was opened. ⁶Out of the sanctuary came the seven angels with the seven plagues, dressed in clean, bright linen, with gold sashes wrapped around their chests. ⁷One of the four living creatures gave the seven angels seven gold bowls filled with the wrath of God who lives forever and ever. ⁸Then the sanctuary was filled with smoke from God's glory and from His power, and no one could enter the sanctuary until the seven plagues of the seven angels were completed.

Revelation 15:1–8

QUESTIONS FOR INTERACTION

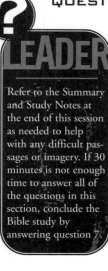

LEADER

Refer to the Summary and Study Notes at the end of this session as needed to help with any difficult passages or imagery. If 30 minutes is not enough time to answer all of the questions in this section, conclude the Bible study by answering question 7.

1. The song in verses 3 and 4 is sung by those who are victorious over the beast. What is the focus of their song? What does this show us about their victory?

2. What does God's holiness mean? How has it been described and demonstrated throughout John's vision so far?

3. Why are the seven angels dressed as they are? What does their appearance suggest about God's wrath?

4. Why does God's glory, which is literally "brightness," give off billows of smoke?

5. Soon, "God's wrath will be completed." How is this encouraging news? What does it tell us about God's plan for eternity?

6. How are God's ways "righteous and true?" When have you experienced this?

7. What "great and awe-inspiring" works has God done in your life?

GOING DEEPER:

If your group has time and/or wants a challenge, go on to this question.

8. Why is no one permitted to enter God's sanctuary until after the seven plagues are completed?

Caring Time   15 Min.

APPLY THE LESSON AND PRAY FOR ONE ANOTHER

LEADER

After sharing together from the following questions and asking for prayer requests, end in a time of group prayer. Pray especially that the Lord will lead you to others who do not know the Gospel.

God's wrath is part of his holiness, and his holiness is both great and terrible. His deeds are all perfect, his works all great and awe-inspiring. Our earthly eyes have trouble seeing this at times, but John has shown us a glimpse of eternity.

1. How is God presently working in your life? Does it feel "not-so-great" at the moment?

2. How are you doing at becoming more holy?

3. Spend extra time in prayer, focusing on God's attributes.

Next Week

This week we caught a glimpse of God's complete holiness, and recognized that at times it includes a holy wrath. In the coming week, spend time in prayer meditating on God's attributes and worshiping him. Next week the seven angels that we met here will pour out their golden bowls of wrath on the earth.

Notes on Revelation 15:1–8

SUMMARY: The seven seals have been opened (6:1–17; 8:1), the seven trumpets have been sounded (8:2–9:21; 11:14–19); now the seven bowls are about to be poured out. The bowls appear to be the contents of the seventh trumpet. They may also be the third woe of Revelation 11:14.

15:1 *another great and awe-inspiring sign.* This is the third such portent. The first was the sign of the radiant woman (12:1); the second that of the red dragon (12:3). In each case, these are events that disclose great meaning. In this case, it is the fact of divine judgment against all that is amiss in the universe. *the seven last plagues.* This is the third and final set of calamities. *with them, God's wrath will be completed.* This seems to mean that with the bowls, this threefold cycle of calamities has ended; God's warning to the world of the impending final judgment is complete. The concept of the wrath of God is found more often in Revelation than any other book of the Bible (vv. 1,7; 12:12; 14:10,19; 16:1,19; 19:15).

15:2–4 Once more John sees an event that will, in fact, happen after the Day of Judgment. In this case, it is a vision of the martyrs slain by the beast, standing around a heavenly sea, singing the song of the Lamb. This is a brief interlude prior to the unfolding of the events of the bowls.

15:2 *sea of glass.* This is like the crystal sea spread out before the throne of God which John saw in his vision described in 4:6. *mixed with fire.* This may refer to the fact that this is now a time of judgment; it may refer to the death of the assembled martyrs; or it may simply be a detail that has no symbolic content. *those who had won the victory.* They won over the demands of the beast (13:15–17) by refusing to disown the name of Christ, by remaining steadfast in their faith, and by refusing to worship the beast or receive his mark (14:12). They died instead, and so frustrated the purposes of the beast. *harps.* Harps are instruments used in the praise of God (5:8; 14:2; Ps. 81:2).

15:3 The first four lines of this hymn are a good example of the structural patterns of Hebrew poetry. The third line restates in different words the essence of the first line; the fourth line does the same for the second line. *the song of … Moses.* There is probably only one song, not two. The song that was sung when the Israelites were delivered out of the hands of the Egyptians (Ex. 15:1–18) is of the same character (similar phrases are found in both) as the one which is sung here concerning this greater deliverance. *the song of the Lamb.* This is the song that follows. It praises God who delivered them from the beast. ***Great and awe-inspiring are Your works.*** This is a common theme in the Old Testament (Ps. 92:5; 111:2; 139:14). ***Lord God, the Almighty.*** God is called Almighty nine times in Revelation and only once in the rest of the New Testament (2 Cor. 6:18). This is appropriate, since his overwhelming power is a central feature in this book.

15:4 A rhetorical question is now raised in the first two lines of this verse. The final three lines all begin in Greek with "for" and cite three reasons why it is inconceivable that God is not feared and honored. ***all the nations will come.*** The fellowship of those who belong to the Lamb includes peoples from all nations.

15:5–8 The final plagues are about to begin.

15:5 *the tabernacle of testimony.* This is how the heavenly temple is described. This is a reference to the tabernacle in the wilderness. It is called the "Tent of the Testimony" in Numbers 17:7 and 18:2 because this is where the two tablets were lodged that Moses brought down from Mt. Sinai (Ex. 32:15–16; Deut. 10:4–5). The "Tent of the Testimony" was to be a copy of the heavenly temple that we see here (Heb. 8:5).

15:6 *Out of the sanctuary came the seven angels with the seven plagues.* The point is that the source of these impending calamities is God himself. *clean, bright linen/gold sashes.* The angels' appearance emphasizes their purity: the wrath of God is holy and spotless.

15:7 *bowls.* A wide, shallow drinking bowl. *who lives forever and ever.* This is a reminder that, although evil may seem to be overwhelming (and indeed it would be for those living under the beast), in fact it is God alone who is eternal and who will prevail.

15:8 *filled with smoke from God's glory.* When God appeared in the Old Testament, there was often smoke (Ex. 19:18; Isa. 6:4). "Glory" suggests light or radiance; yet here again John emphasizes that God's glory also includes his holy wrath (smoke, fire) against man's wickedness.

The Seven Bowls
REVELATION 16:1–21

Last Week

Last session we looked upon the glory of God, surrounded by the saints who will sing his praises for all eternity. We also considered that his wrath is holy, and that all he does is perfect and just. This will be an important point for us this week, as we watch yet again how his holy wrath is poured out upon mankind, always with the purpose of bringing men and women to repentance.

Ice-Breaker   15 Min.
CONNECT WITH YOUR GROUP

LEADER

Choose one or two of the Ice-Breaker questions. If you have a new group member you may want to do all three. Remember to stick closely to the three-part agenda and the time allowed for each segment.

Travel, they say, is "broadening." It does afford one the opportunity of seeing and doing things that are totally foreign to our previous experience. And sometimes it can bring better insight into God's word. Take a few minutes to get to know one another with the following questions.

1. What great bodies of water have you seen? Did you swim in them?

   ○ Atlantic Ocean.
   ○ Pacific Ocean.
   ○ Indian Ocean.
   ○ Mediterranean Sea.
   ○ Other _____.

2. What is the hottest place you've ever visited?

3. Have you ever experienced complete darkness, such as in a cave? What was it like?

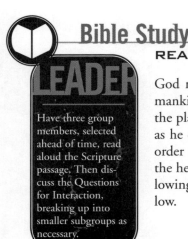

Bible Study   30 Min.

LEADER

Have three group members, selected ahead of time, read aloud the Scripture passage. Then discuss the Questions for Interaction, breaking up into smaller subgroups as necessary.

God now has his angels pour forth the bowls of his wrath upon mankind, bringing about seven plagues which are reminiscent of the plagues upon the Egyptians before the Exodus of the Jews. Just as he did with the Egyptians, so here God brings these plagues in order to move men to repentance; but, just as with the Egyptians, the hearts of all mankind are hard and will not bend. Read the following passage from Revelation, then discuss the questions that follow.

The Seven Bowls

Reader One: 16 Then I heard a loud voice from the sanctuary saying to the seven angels, "Go and pour out the seven bowls of God's wrath on the earth." ²The first went and poured out his bowl on the earth, and severely painful sores broke out on the people who had the mark of the beast and who worshiped his image.

³The second poured out his bowl into the sea. It turned to blood like a dead man's, and all life in the sea died.

⁴The third poured out his bowl into the rivers and the springs of water, and they became blood. ⁵I heard the angel of the waters say:

Reader Two: You are righteous, who is and who was, the Holy One,
  for You have decided these things.
⁶Because they poured out the blood of the saints and the prophets,
  You also gave them blood to drink; they deserve it!
⁷Then I heard someone from the altar say:
  Yes, Lord God, the Almighty,
  true and righteous are Your judgments.

Reader Three: ⁸The fourth poured out his bowl on the sun. He was given the power to burn people with fire, ⁹and people were burned by the intense heat. So they blasphemed the name of God who had the power over these plagues, and they did not repent and give Him glory.

¹⁰The fifth poured out his bowl on the throne of the beast, and his kingdom was plunged into darkness. People gnawed their tongues from pain ¹¹and blasphemed the God of heaven because of their pains and their sores, yet they did not repent of their actions.

Reader One: ¹²The sixth poured out his bowl on the great river Euphrates, and its water was dried up to prepare the way for the kings from the east. ¹³Then I saw three unclean spirits like frogs coming from the dragon's mouth, from the beast's mouth, and from the mouth of the false prophet. [14]For they are spirits of demons performing signs, who travel to the kings of the whole world to assemble them for the battle of the great day of God, the Almighty.

[15]"Look, I am coming like a thief. Blessed is the one who is alert and remains clothed so that he may not go naked, and they see his shame."

Reader Two: [16]So they assembled them at the place called in Hebrew Armagedon.

[17]Then the seventh poured out his bowl into the air, and a loud voice came out of the sanctuary, from the throne, saying, "It is done!" [18]There were lightnings, rumblings, and thunders. And a severe earthquake occurred like no other since man has been on the earth—so great was the quake. [19]The great city split into three parts, and the cities of the nations fell. Babylon the Great was remembered in God's presence; He gave her the cup filled with the wine of His fierce anger. [20]Every island fled, and the mountains disappeared. [21]Enormous hailstones, each weighing about 100 pounds, fell from heaven on the people, and they blasphemed God for the plague of hail because that plague was extremely severe.

Revelation 16:1–21

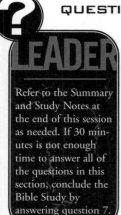

QUESTIONS FOR INTERACTION

1. Scan Exodus 7–12 and compare the plagues in Egypt with those described here. How are they similar? How are they different?

2. Why is a person blessed if he "is alert and remains clothed?" What does this mean? How does it parallel the first Passover in Exodus 12?

3. What do these plagues represent? How might such things (intensification of the sun's heat, water turned to blood, etc.) come about?

Refer to the Summary and Study Notes at the end of this session as needed. If 30 minutes is not enough time to answer all of the questions in this section, conclude the Bible Study by answering question 7.

4. Who is in control of these plagues? Why is he pouring them out?

5. What is mankind's response? How might a different response have changed things?

6. Why does the angel say that the people of earth deserve such harsh judgments? Do you think that we deserve these things?

7. Why are these judgments on mankind particularly appropriate? What does this say about your own life?

GOING DEEPER:

If your group has time and/or wants a challenge, go on to this question.

8. What is the meaning of God's pronouncement, "It is done"? Why is God the only one who can utter such a statement?

Caring Time   15 Min.

APPLY THE LESSON AND PRAY FOR ONE ANOTHER

God sent plagues and suffering to the Egyptians when they would not obey his command to let the Israelites go. He sends suffering upon all mankind in order that we might repent and turn back to him. The fact is, all people deserve to be cast away from God, for there is no righteousness in anyone apart from the righteousness of Christ.

1. If God gave you what you deserve, what would your life be like?

2. Are you alert and clothed? If not, how can this group help?

3. Spend extra time in prayer, thanking God that he has not given us what we deserve, but he has given us that which we could never deserve. Pray also for those in your life whose names are not written in the book of life.

Next Week

This week we watched as God poured out his wrath upon the earth, seeing horrible suffering and death. But we were reminded again that his purpose is always to draw all men to himself, and his wrath is intended to bring people to repentance. In the coming week, spend time alone with God to thank him for his mercy and grace, and ask him if there are any areas in your life where you need to repent. Next week we will meet the woman named Babylon, the great prostitute.

Notes on Revelation 16:1–21

SUMMARY: The whole of chapter 16 is given over to the emptying of the bowls. The parallels are clear between the plagues here and those that followed the trumpets. In each series, the first four plagues come upon earth, sea, fresh water, and heavenly bodies in that order. The fifth plagues both have to do with great pain; the sixth brought invasions from across the Euphrates. Both sets of plagues parallel the plagues in Egypt. One major difference between the trumpet plagues and the bowl plagues is their intensity. While the trumpet plagues were limited (usually they affected only a third), the bowl plagues encompass the whole. A second difference is that the first four trumpet plagues fall on the land, while the first four bowl plagues directly affect mankind.

16:2 The first plague falls upon those who bear the mark of the beast, marking them with loathsome boils. This plague parallels the sixth Egyptian plague in the Old Testament (Ex. 9:8–11).

16:4 The third plague did the same to all the fresh water. There would thus be no water to drink in the land. This parallels the third trumpet plague (8:10–11).

16:5–6 An angel breaks in on this unrelenting unfolding of tragedy in order to attest to the righteness of God in doing this.

16:6 The fact that God turned the waters to blood is not a capricious act on God's part. Because the followers of the beast had been like bloodthirsty animals in pouring out the blood of the saints, God is giving them blood to drink as their judgment.

16:9 *they blasphemed the name of God.* They know full well who is behind these calamities. *they did not repent.* Even at this point, it seems, repentance is possible. Still, they will not turn to God. Like Pharaoh, who saw the plagues and yet would not change, their hearts are hard.

16:10–11 The fifth plague directly attacks the heart of the problem. It assaults the throne of the beast and plunges his kingdom into darkness. This darkness parallels the ninth Egyptian plague (Ex. 10:21–29).

16:11 *their pains.* This may be a result of the heat from the scorching sun. *their sores.* The sores

(which they received as a result of the first plague) continue to afflict them. In other words, the impact of the plagues build one upon another to the climactic act of judgment. *they did not repent.* Still they hold out against God.

16:12–16 The sixth plague dries up the great river Euphrates. Since it is no longer a barrier, an invasion is planned (Ex. 14:21; Josh. 3:14–17). The sixth trumpet plague was also centered on the Euphrates. This plague is different from the others in that it does not directly bring suffering to people. It does, however, pave the way for war.

16:12 *kings from the East.* The identity of these kings is unknown. One commentator noted that there have been nearly 50 different interpretations of who they are.

16:13 *frogs.* In the second Egyptian plague, frogs overran the land (Ex. 8:1–15). *false prophet.* This is the first time this name is used. It refers to the second beast in 13:11–17. Both Jesus and Paul warned about false prophets who would arise in the last days and seek to lead people astray (Matt. 24:24; 2 Thess. 2:9–10).

16:16 The narrative of the sixth bowl continues. The demonic spirits gather the kings for the battle which will be described in 19:11–21. The idea of a last great battle between God's people and the forces hostile to God is mentioned throughout Scripture (Ps. 2:2–3; Isa. 5:26–30; Jer. 6:1–5; Ezek. 38; Joel 3:9–16). *Armagedon.* In Hebrew, this word means "the mountains of Megiddo."

However, in Palestine, Megiddo is a plain that stretches from the Sea of Galilee to the Mediterranean, so it is not clear where, precisely, this is. The region of Megiddo was the site of many battles in the history of Israel (Judg. 5:19; 2 Kin. 9:27; 23:29; 2 Chron. 35:22).

16:19 The city of the beast is undone, as are the cities of those who aligned themselves with the beast. See 17:12–14 and 18:9 for details of this event. *remembered in God's presence.* During the short reign of the Antichrist, it might have appeared as if God had forgotten the wicked city and his people who lived there. But he had not. It was just a matter of time and patient endurance. Now Babylon will receive its due. *the cup filled with the wine of His fierce anger.* Babylon caused the nations to drink from the cup of her fornication and they grew rich from this adultery (18:3). Now Babylon is forced to drink from another cup—the cup of God's wrath (14:10).

16:21 *plague of hail.* There is a parallel to the seventh Egyptian plague (Ex. 9:13–35).

SESSION 5
The Dragon and the Woman
REVELATION 17:1–18

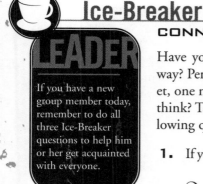

Last Week

Last week we watched as God poured out his seven plagues on the human race, urging men to repent of their sins and turn to him. This week God's wrath will focus specifically on Babylon, the "notorious prostitute" who turned the nations away from God. Babylon will symbolize for us the systems of human society that strive for greatness apart from God.

Ice-Breaker   15 Min.

CONNECT WITH YOUR GROUP

LEADER

If you have a new group member today, remember to do all three Ice-Breaker questions to help him or her get acquainted with everyone.

Have you ever wished that you could change the world in some way? Perhaps, if one could only be absolute monarch over the planet, one might be able to accomplish some great good. What do you think? Take a few minutes to get to know one another with the following questions.

1. If you could rule the world for just one hour, what would you do?

- ○ Cancel taxes.
- ○ Buy lots of things.
- ○ Kill my enemies.
- ○ Stop all clocks to make that hour last.
- ○ Other _____.

2. What is your favorite precious stone?
- ○ Diamonds.
- ○ Sapphires.
- ○ Rubies.
- ○ Emeralds.
- ○ Other _____.

3. What is one of your favorite books, and why?

READ SCRIPTURE AND DISCUSS

Have four group members, whom you have selected beforehand, read the following passage from Revelation. Then discuss the Questions for Interaction, dividing into smaller subgroups as necessary.

This week we meet Babylon, the "notorious prostitute" who seduced the nations to join in her blasphemous immoralities. Babylon, a great ancient city, represents man's system of life on earth when he strives to become great and wealthy and powerful by himself, denying the power and authority of God. In the process of building this great city, Babylon has trampled on the people of God, bringing down his fierce wrath upon them. Read the following passage from Revelation, then discuss the questions that follow.

The Dragon and the Woman

Reader One:
17 Then one of the seven angels who had the seven bowls came and spoke with me: "Come, I will show you the judgment of the notorious prostitute who sits on many waters. ²The kings of the earth committed sexual immorality with her, and those who live on the earth became drunk on the wine of her sexual immorality." ³So he carried me away in the Spirit to a desert. I saw a woman sitting on a scarlet beast that was covered with blasphemous names, having seven heads and 10 horns. ⁴The woman was dressed in purple and scarlet, adorned with gold, precious stones, and pearls. She had a gold cup in her hand filled with everything vile and with the impurities of her prostitution. ⁵On her forehead a cryptic name was written:

BABYLON THE GREAT
THE MOTHER OF PROSTITUTES
AND OF THE VILE THINGS OF THE EARTH

Reader Two:
⁶Then I saw that the woman was drunk on the blood of the saints and on the blood of the witnesses to Jesus. When I saw her, I was utterly astounded.

⁷Then the angel said to me, "Why are you astounded? I will tell you the secret meaning of the woman and of the beast, with the seven heads and the 10 horns, that carries her. ⁸The beast that you saw was, and is not, and is about to come up from the abyss and go to destruction. Those who live on the earth whose names were not written in the book of life from the foundation of the world will be astounded when they see the beast that was, and is not, and will be present again.

Reader Three:
⁹"Here is the mind with wisdom: the seven heads are seven mountains on which the woman is seated. ¹⁰They are also seven kings: five have fallen, one is, the other has not yet come, and when he comes, he must remain for a little while. ¹¹The beast that was and is not, is himself the eighth, yet is of the seven and goes to destruction. ¹²The

10 horns you saw are 10 kings who have not yet received a kingdom, but they will receive authority as kings with the beast for one hour. ¹³These have one purpose, and they give their power and authority to the beast. ¹⁴These will make war against the Lamb, but the Lamb will conquer them because he is Lord of lords and King of kings. Those with him are called and elect and faithful."

Reader Four: ¹⁵He also said to me, "The waters you saw, where the prostitute was seated, are peoples, multitudes, nations, and languages. ¹⁶The 10 horns you saw, and the beast, will hate the prostitute. They will make her desolate and naked, devour her flesh, and burn her up with fire. ¹⁷For God has put it into their hearts to carry out His plan by having one purpose, and to give their kingdom to the beast until God's words are accomplished. ¹⁸And the woman you saw is the great city that has an empire over the kings of the earth."

Revelation 17:1–18

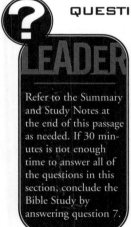

QUESTIONS FOR INTERACTION

Refer to the Summary and Study Notes at the end of this passage as needed. If 30 minutes is not enough time to answer all of the questions in this section, conclude the Bible Study by answering question 7.

1. Describe the appearance of the "notorious prostitute." What does this appearance suggest about her?

2. What characterizes the reigns of the 10 kings (vv. 9–14)? What is their "purpose?"

3. What does John suggest when he says that the great kingdoms of man have a "purpose?"

4. Who will defeat these kings, and why? What does this tell us about the true nature of human history?

5. Why do the beast and the great kings hate the prostitute if they all do the work of Satan? What does this show us of the true nature of man's wickedness?

6. Whose plan is actually being accomplished by the deeds of the wicked? What is his purpose?

7. Who or what might be like the "notorious prostitute" in today's world? In your own life?

If your group has time and/or wants a challenge, go on to this question.

8. What does it mean that "Babylon the Great" is "the mother of prostitutes?" How can a kingdom or city or society become the mother "of the vile things of the earth?"

Caring Time   15 Min.

APPLY THE LESSON AND PRAY FOR ONE ANOTHER

We live in a war zone, and our enemy is ever alert to destroy us. Satan uses anything he can find to lure us away from our devotion to God, to help us harden our hearts against God's call to repentance.

1. Is there something in your life at present that makes it difficult for you to remain faithful to God? How can the group support you?

2. Are you among the Lamb's "called and elect and faithful?"

3. How can the group pray for you during the next week?

Next Week

This week we were confronted with the fact that mankind, apart from God, cannot hope to produce anything that is lasting and undefiled. Our best works apart from God are like a prostitute's sexual immorality. In the coming week, ask God to lead you into his plan, helping you to focus on the things that he would have you be doing, instead of letting your life get filled up with the things of this world. Next week we will witness the final, devastating fall of Babylon the Great.

SUMMARY: The book of Revelation is now coming to its conclusion. A great vision of judgment is shown to John, and the focus is shifted to the overthrow of the wicked. This chapter is about the great prostitute, Babylon, and her demise.

17:1 For the third time, John is invited to behold a vision (1:9–11; 4:1–2; 21:9–10). *sits on many waters.* The Babylon of history was built on a network of canals (Jer. 51:13). John interprets the meaning of these "many waters" in 17:15 as "peoples, multitudes, nations, and languages."

17:2 *sexual immorality.* In this context, this term describes the corrupting influence of Babylon which enticed the nations to prostitute everything for the sake of riches, luxury, and pleasure (Isa. 23:16–17; Jer. 51:7; Nah. 3:4). *those who live on the earth.* The people followed their rulers and joined in this orgy.

17:3 The angel then takes John into the wilderness. *in the Spirit.* John is in the midst of a vision (1:10; 4:2). *a scarlet beast.* The same beast as in 13:1, the Antichrist. His scarlet color identifies him with his master, Satan, the red dragon (12:3). It is the beast who has made the city (the harlot) great. She rides upon him. *blasphemous names.* See 13:5–6.

17:4 *purple and scarlet.* The high cost of these dyes made clothing of this color expensive, so that it could only be worn by the wealthy. *gold, precious stones, and pearls.* She is opulently dressed. *gold cup.* One would expect it to be filled with the finest wine. *everything vile.* Instead it contains that which is foul and detestable (Jer. 51:7).

17:5 *on her forehead.* Prostitutes in Rome wore headbands bearing the name of their owners. *THE MOTHER OF PROSTITUTES.* Not content simply to pursue her own adulteries, she made her daughters into harlots; she has spread her corruption throughout the world.

17:7–18 The angel will now proceed to interpret the meaning of what John has seen.

17:8 *was, and is not, and is about to come up from the abyss.* A description that mimics that of the Lamb (1:18; 2:8). *destruction.* Literally, perdition, the state of final doom (Matt. 7:13).

17:9 *seven mountains.* A traditional view is that this describes Rome (the city built on seven hills). Whatever one concludes, most likely John's readers would think of Rome. In terms of the total vision, however, no simple identification with any single historical city is possible.

17:10 *seven kings.* The identity of these kings has been hotly debated, since they cannot easily be lined up with the actual succession of Roman emperors. Some scholars take the number 7 to represent (as it often does in Revelation) the fullness of imperial power so that the seven kings stand for a succession of kingdoms. The key thing, however, is that this power is drawing to an end.

17:11 The eighth king is identified by some as the Antichrist (Dan. 7:24) or as specific world leaders depending upon the times. This is a difficult verse. A possibility is that the seventh king with the short reign will reappear a second time as the eighth king (who is therefore one of the seven) and will be a particularly virulent manifestation of the beast. We will only know with the fulfillment of the prophecy.

17:12 The 10 horns are identified as 10 kings (Dan. 7:7,24). Many guesses have been made as to the identity of these 10. *not yet received a kingdom.* Whoever these men are, they are not Roman emperors, since they do not yet possess kingdoms. *one hour.* A short time.

17:13 They are completely devoted to the beast. They seek his ends, not their own.

17:14 They are even willing to fight against the Lamb. This final conflict at Armageddon will be discussed in 19:11–21. *because he is Lord of lords and King of kings.* Given the nature of the Messiah's sovereign power as captured in this title, the outcome of the battle is certain (19:16; Deut. 10:17; Ps. 136:2–3; Dan. 2:47). His victory will be shared by those who have remained faithful to him even to the point of death.

17:15 The harlot is defined as the city which rules over many nations.

17:16 Here John describes how Babylon is destroyed. The harlot draws her power from the beast (v. 3) and, in turn, supports the beast in his plans (v. 13). However, the beast—along with the 10 kings—turns on the harlot, destroying her with great viciousness. No reason is given for this action. A league of evil ultimately turns against itself. *hate the prostitute.* They bear her no love for what she has done for them and to them. *make her desolate and naked.* All her fine clothes and wonderful jewels will be taken from her (v. 4). *devour her flesh.* See 2 Kin. 9:30–37. *burn her up with fire.* See Leviticus 21:9.

17:17 John explains this surprising turn of events. It is God who has ordered that the harlot be brought to destruction.

SESSION 6
The Fall of Babylon
REVELATION 18:1–24

Last Week

We met Babylon last week, the "notorious prostitute" who seduced the nations away from God. This week we will witness the city's final destruction, and we will discover the true reactions of the people of earth.

Ice-Breaker   15 Min.

CONNECT WITH YOUR GROUP

This week we will watch as all the people of the earth react to the fall of Babylon, discussing the things they'd purchased there and the ways they had done business with the city. Just about anything anyone could want could be purchased there, and every form of transportation was used to move the goods. Take a few minutes to get to know one another with the following questions.

1. If you could be captain of a ship, what type would you choose?

2. What is your favorite fruit?

3. What is your favorite city? Least favorite?

Bible Study   30 Min.

READ SCRIPTURE AND DISCUSS

Last week we met the "notorious prostitute" Babylon and were told of her great sins. This week we will witness her final destruction, and will listen as all the people of the world make comment upon it. Their comments will be quite revealing, and may surprise us as to how people truly felt about the great city. Read the following passage from Revelation, then discuss the questions that follow.

The Fall of Babylon

Reader One:

18 After this I saw another angel with great authority coming down from heaven, and the earth was illuminated by his splendor. ²He cried in a mighty voice:

It has fallen, Babylon the Great has fallen!
She has become a dwelling for demons,
a haunt for every unclean spirit,
a haunt for every unclean bird,
and a haunt for every unclean and despicable beast.
³For all the nations have drunk
the wine of her sexual immorality, which brings wrath.
The kings of the earth have committed sexual immorality with her,
and the merchants of the earth have grown wealthy from her excessive luxury.

Reader Two: ⁴Then I heard another voice from heaven:

Come out of her, My people,
so that you will not share in her sins,
or receive any of her plagues.
⁵For her sins are piled up to heaven,
and God has remembered her crimes.
⁶Pay her back the way she also paid,
and double it according to her works.
In the cup in which she mixed,
mix a double portion for her.
⁷As much as she glorified herself and lived luxuriously,
give her that much torment and grief.
Because she says in her heart, 'I sit as queen;
I am not a widow, and I will never see grief,'
⁸therefore her plagues will come in one day—
death, and grief, and famine.
She will be burned up with fire,
because the Lord God who judges her is mighty.

Reader Three: ⁹The kings of the earth who have committed sexual immorality and lived luxuriously with her will weep and mourn over her when they see the smoke of her burning. ¹⁰They stand far off in fear of her torment, saying:

Woe, woe, the great city,
Babylon, the mighty city!
For in a single hour
your judgment has come.

¹¹The merchants of the earth will also weep and mourn over her, because no one buys their merchandise any longer— ¹²merchandise of gold, silver, precious stones, and pearls; fine fabrics of linen, purple, silk, and scarlet; all kinds of fragrant wood products; objects of ivory; objects of expensive wood, brass, iron, and marble; ¹³cinnamon, spice, incense, myrrh, and frankincense; wine, olive oil, fine wheat flour, and grain; cattle and sheep; horses and carriages; and human bodies and souls.

Reader One: [14]The fruit you craved has left you.

All your splendid and glamorous things are gone;

they will never find them again.

[15]The merchants of these things, who became rich from her, will stand far off in fear of her torment, weeping and mourning, [16]saying:

Woe, woe, the great city,

clothed in fine linen, purple, and scarlet,

adorned with gold, precious stones, and pearls;

[17]because in a single hour such fabulous wealth was destroyed!

Reader Two: And every shipmaster, seafarer, the sailors, and all who do business by sea, stood far off [18]as they watched the smoke from her burning and kept crying out: "Who is like the great city?" [19]They threw dust on their heads and kept crying out, weeping, and mourning:

Woe, woe, the great city,

where all those who have ships on the sea

became rich from her wealth;

because in a single hour she was destroyed.

[20]Rejoice over her, heaven, and you saints, apostles, and prophets,

because God has executed your judgment on her!

Reader Three: [21]Then a mighty angel picked up a stone like a large millstone and threw it into the sea, saying:

In this way, Babylon the great city will be thrown down violently

and never be found again.

[22]The sound of harpists, musicians, flutists, and trumpeters

will never be heard in you again;

no craftsman of any trade

will ever be found in you again;

the sound of a mill

will never be heard in you again;

[23]the light of a lamp will never shine in you again;

and the voice of a groom and bride

will never be heard in you again.

All this will happen

because your merchants were the nobility of the earth,

because all the nations were deceived by your sorcery,

[24]and the blood of prophets and saints,

and all those slaughtered on earth, was found in you.

Revelation 18:1–24

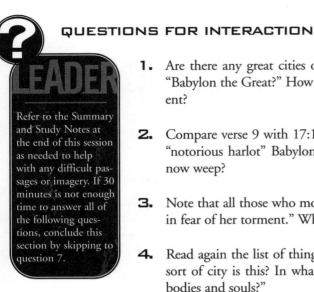

QUESTIONS FOR INTERACTION

Refer to the Summary and Study Notes at the end of this session as needed to help with any difficult passages or imagery. If 30 minutes is not enough time to answer all of the following questions, conclude this section by skipping to question 7.

1. Are there any great cities or societies today that remind you of "Babylon the Great?" How are they similar? How are they different?

2. Compare verse 9 with 17:16. If the kings of the earth hated the "notorious harlot" Babylon and destroyed her, why would they now weep?

3. Note that all those who mourn the loss of Babylon "stand far off in fear of her torment." What does this reveal about their grief?

4. Read again the list of things bought and sold in Babylon. What sort of city is this? In what ways might a city trade in "human bodies and souls?"

5. What does it mean for God's people to "come out of" Babylon? What does this command mean to us today?

6. One of Babylon's sins is that "she glorified herself and lived luxuriously." How do we risk glorifying ourselves? Do we live luxuriously?

7. Do you think that our country has any of Babylon's traits?

GOING DEEPER:

If your group has time and/or wants a challenge, go on to this question.

8. Might the modern idea of striving to love oneself be an example of Babylon's sin of glorifying herself? How might learning to love oneself lead to living luxuriously?

Caring Time

APPLY THE LESSON AND PRAY FOR ONE ANOTHER

LEADER

Be sure to save at least 15 minutes for this time of prayer and encouragement. Continue to encourage group members to invite new people to the group.

Babylon represents mankind's attempts to find fulfillment apart from God, seeking material comforts, power and pleasure. As followers of Christ, however, we are commanded to "come out" of that way of thinking and be different.

1. Do you need to "come out" of Babylon? If so, what needs to change?

2. Do you find that it is difficult to put God or others ahead of yourself? What makes it difficult?

3. How can the group support you in prayer this week?

Next Week

In this passage, we were challenged by God to "come out" of Babylon, to live very differently from the world around us. Our strength and security cannot be found in any of man's systems or schemes, but only in learning to love God above all else and obey him at any cost. In the coming week, ask the Lord to show you any ways in which he might have you "come out" of the world's ways of thinking and be changed to his way of thinking. Next week we will listen to heaven's great Hallelujah Chorus!

Notes on Revelation 18:1–24

SUMMARY: First, the fall of the city is announced by an angel. Then God's people are warned against getting trapped by her seductive powers. They are urged to flee from Babylon, lest they share in her coming destruction (Isa. 52:11; Jer. 51:45). A great lament goes up from the kings and the merchants and the seafarers over the destruction of Babylon. These were the people who profited by their relationship with her. Their cries are not over the city herself, but over the loss of their power and profit. The cry of "Woe!" is repeated three times (vv. 10,16,19).

18:2 The language used to describe the fall of this Babylon is similar to the language used to describe the fall of Babylon in the Old Testament, as well as the fall of Edom and Nineveh (Isa. 34:11–15; Zeph. 2:15). *Babylon the Great has fallen!* These are the very words of the second angel in 14:8 (Isa. 21:9). *a haunt.* See Isaiah 13:21–22.

18:3 *For.* The reason for the fall of Babylon is that she has corrupted the nations of the earth. *committed sexual immorality with her.* This is a term used in the Old Testament to describe spiritual unfaithfulness on the part of the people of Israel (Isa. 1:21; Jer. 2:20–30; 3:1; Ezek. 16:15; Hos. 2:5; 4:15). She has seduced the nations to follow the beast. What she used was the lure of riches and luxury.

18:7 *I am not a widow, and I will never see grief.* Babylon is so secure in her power and invincibility that she boasts in this way. She denies that her armies will die on the battlefield. Others may experience loss, but she will not (Isa. 47:7–9). Her self-deception will end with her fall, however.

18:12–13 The 29 items are divided into seven types of merchandise: precious minerals, fabrics used for expensive clothing, ornamental decorations, aromatic substances, food, animals, and slaves. Fifteen of the items in this catalog of imports are mentioned in the lament over the destruction of Tyre, another great trading nation (Ezek. 27).

18:12 *gold.* This was mined by slaves under the lash. *fine fabrics of linen.* A very costly fabric, woven so fine as to be virtually transparent. It was popular in women's fashion. *purple.* Purple dye was imported from Phoenicia. It was rare and

expensive, since it was extracted drop by drop from a small vein in certain shellfish. *silk.* Silk came from China and was very expensive. A pound of silk was equal in value to a pound of gold. *scarlet.* This was made from another expensive dye. *expensive wood.* Citron was a dark, luxurious wood from North Africa that was very scarce and was used to make expensive furniture.

18:13 *cinnamon.* This spice came from South China and was used as a fragrance (Prov. 7:17). *spice.* This does not refer to spices used in cooking, but to a perfume used in the hair. *myrrh.* This was used as a medicine, as a perfume, and in embalming. *frankincense.* A gum resin from a tree used as a perfume and for flavoring wine. *carriages.* These were a form of chariot used by the wealthy. *human bodies and souls.* There was a flourishing slave trade. It was estimated that in the first century there were 60 million slaves who held jobs that ranged from the menial to the exalted, including servants, teachers, physicians, civil servants, etc.

18:17 *stood far off.* They lament the loss but separate themselves from the city, lest they get caught in the destruction.

18:22 *The sound of harpists, musicians, flutists, and trumpeters.* Babylon was known as a great patron of the arts. Flutes were used for festivals and funerals (Isa. 30:29; Matt. 9:23). Trumpets were sounded at the games and in the theater.

18:24 *all those slaughtered on earth.* The influence of Babylon has spread throughout the land, so it can be said that in her is found the blood of all the martyrs.

SESSION 7
Hallelujah!
REVELATION 19:1–10

Last Week

Last week we watched as the great city Babylon was destroyed, and listened to the self-centered laments of the world. This week we will listen to something quite different: the Christ-centered praises of all creation before the throne of God, the greatest of all Hallelujah choruses!

Ice-Breaker   15 Min.

CONNECT WITH YOUR GROUP

LEADER

Introduce and welcome new group members. If there are no new members, choose one or two of the Ice-Breaker questions to get started. If there are new members, then discuss all three.

Weddings are probably the most important and memorable occasion of anyone's life. But sometimes they can be memorable for unexpected reasons. What was your own wedding like? Take a few minutes to get to know one another with the following questions.

1. If you are married, what were your own wedding preparations like?

    ○ Well-organized in advance.
    ○ Chaotic and last-minute.
    ○ Minimal and relaxed.
    ○ Totally pointless.
    ○ Other _____.

2. What is the most romantic or unusual marriage proposal you've ever heard of?

3. What was the most memorable wedding or reception you ever attended?

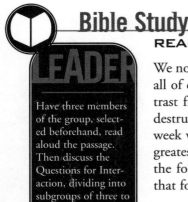

We now turn our attention back to the throne of God, and listen as all of creation sings their hallelujahs to the Almighty. What a contrast from the selfish laments of the nations, as they watched the destruction of Babylon and thought only of their own losses. This week we will gather together to prepare ourselves to partake of the greatest wedding feast of all time, the marriage of the Lamb. Read the following passage from Revelation, then discuss the questions that follow.

Have three members of the group, selected beforehand, read aloud the passage. Then discuss the Questions for Interaction, dividing into subgroups of three to six.

Hallelujah!

Reader One: 19 After this I heard something like the loud voice of a vast multitude in heaven, saying:

> Hallelujah!
> Salvation, glory, and power belong to our God,
> [2]because His judgments are true and righteous,
> because He has judged the notorious prostitute
> who corrupted the earth with her sexual immorality;
> and He has avenged the blood of His servants that was on her hands.

Reader Two: [3]A second time they said:

> Hallelujah!
> Her smoke ascends forever and ever!

[4]Then the 24 elders and the four living creatures fell down and worshiped God, who is seated on the throne, saying:

> Amen! Hallelujah!

[5]A voice came from the throne, saying:

> Praise our God,
> all you His servants, you who fear Him,
> both small and great!

Reader Three: [6]Then I heard something like the voice of a vast multitude, like the sound of cascading waters, and like the rumbling of loud thunder, saying:

> Hallelujah—because our Lord God, the Almighty,
> has begun to reign!
> [7]Let us be glad, rejoice, and give Him glory,
> because the marriage of the Lamb has come,
> and His wife has prepared herself.
> [8]She was permitted to wear fine linen, bright and pure

For the fine linen represents the righteous acts of the saints.

⁹Then he said to me, "Write: Blessed are those invited to the marriage feast of the Lamb!" He also said to me, "These words of God are true." ¹⁰Then I fell at his feet to worship him, but he said to me, "Don't do that! I am a fellow slave with you and your brothers who have the testimony about Jesus. Worship God, because the testimony about Jesus is the spirit of prophecy."

Revelation 19:1–10

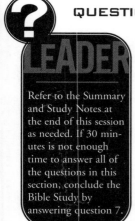

QUESTIONS FOR INTERACTION

1. Why is the first hallelujah chorus focused on rejoicing over the destruction of the "notorious prostitute," whose "smoke ascends forever and ever?" Why would heaven praise God for his acts of wrath and judgment?

Refer to the Summary and Study Notes at the end of this session as needed. If 30 minutes is not enough time to answer all of the questions in this section, conclude the Bible Study by answering question 7.

2. Contrast the prostitute of chapters 17 and 18 with the bride of verses 6–9. (See also Eph. 5:25–27.) What do you find interesting about this contrast?

3. How has the wife of the Lamb "prepared herself" for this marriage? How can we be preparing ourselves?

4. Note that the wife is "permitted" to wear fine linen. What does this suggest about our "righteous acts?" About God's grace?

5. Who are the blessed people who are invited to the marriage feast of the Lamb? Are you one of the blessed?

6. What does this passage tell you about what we should be focusing on now?

7. How is marriage symbolic of the relationship between Jesus and his church? What should this cause us to do?

GOING DEEPER:

If your group has time and/or wants a challenge, go to this question.

8. Why is John tempted to worship the angel? Do you see this tendency in society today? The tendency to "worship" other messengers of God?

♥ Caring Time   15 Min.

LEADER

Continue to encourage group members to invite new people to the group. Remind everyone that this group is for learning and sharing, but also for reaching out to others. Close the group prayer by thanking God for each member and for this time together.

All mankind will be resurrected to stand before God, but not all will partake of the great wedding feast. Only those whose names are written in the book of life will be among the blessed. But even those who are born again must continue to prepare themselves for the great wedding feast.

1. Where do you see yourself in this unfolding picture? In what group do you belong: on the wedding list or not?

2. How well are you doing on your "bridal preparations" this week?

3. How can the group support you in prayer in the coming week?

Next Week

This week, we caught a glimpse of the wedding feast of the Lamb, the day of eternal rejoicing which will come for those whose names are written in the book of life. In the coming week, ask the Lord to show you what preparations he would have you make to get ready for that great day. Next week we will meet our Groom, the rider on the great white horse.

Notes on Revelation 19:1–10

SUMMARY: The story of the destruction of Babylon is concluded by a shout of thanksgiving on the part of the heavenly company. The fall of Babylon and the removal of her corrupting influence is celebrated. This contrasts sharply with the preceding dirges of the kings, merchants, and seafarers who mourn their loss of income. John announces the marriage of the Lamb, though he does not describe it. It is announced here and assumed in later chapters (21:2–3,9–10).

19:1 *Hallelujah!* An exclamation of praise derived from two Hebrew words meaning "Praise the Lord." It is used frequently in the Psalms (Ps. 106; 111–113), though never in the New Testament apart from the four occurrences in this passage (vv. 1,3–4, 6). *Salvation.* Judgment alone is not the point. The fall of Babylon is a necessary part of the grand scheme of salvation. *glory, and power.* Not only was God's salvation displayed in this act, so too was his majesty and might.

19:2 *corrupted the earth.* The influence of Babylon had infected the whole planet. Now it is gone, and so the way has been prepared for the coming of the kingdom.

19:4 The 24 elders and the four living creatures appear for the last time in the book of Revelation. It is fitting that their last cry is "Amen, Hallelujah!"

19:6–21:8 The scene shifts again and John is witness to the final triumph of the Lamb. That which was announced in 11:15 is now enacted.

19:6 Once again, John proclaims an event that is in the future as he did in 11:15 and 14:8. The reign of God in fullness will not actually take place until Jesus returns and the messianic era bursts forth.

19:7 *His wife.* Israel was regularly spoken of as the wife of Yahweh (Isa. 54:5; 62:5; Jer. 31:32; Ezek. 16:8–14; Hos. 2:19–20). Jesus spoke of himself as the bridegroom (Mark 2:19–20), and John the Baptist used this same language to describe Jesus (John 3:29). Jesus also used the idea of the wedding feast in his parables (Matt. 22:1–14; 25:1–13). Paul picks up the idea of Israel as the bride of God and applies it to the church (Rom. 7:1–4; 1 Cor. 6:17; 2 Cor. 11:2; Eph. 5:25–27).

19:8 *permitted to wear.* Her wedding clothes are given to her as a gift. *Fine linen, bright and pure.* This contrasts sharply to the bright robes of the harlot (17:4). The wedding clothes of the bride are similar to the white robes of the martyrs washed in the blood of the lamb (7:14).

19:9 The focus shifts to the wedding guests. In the fluid language of metaphor, the church is both bride and guests. This same fluidity is seen else-where in the New Testament. In Mark 2:19–20, the disciples are pictured as guests at the wedding. Likewise in the parable of the wedding banquet, the bride is not mentioned. The issue there has to do with who the guests will be. However, in Ephesians 5:25–27 the church is spoken of as the bride who is made ready for her husband, Christ. *Blessed.* This is the fourth of the seven beatitudes in Revelation (1:3; 14:13; 16:15; 20:6; 22:7,14). *the marriage feast.* This is the great messianic banquet about which Jesus spoke (Matt. 8:11; 26:29).

19:10 *Then I fell at his feet.* John has encountered angels constantly during his visions, but here he is so overwhelmed by this vision that he falls at the feet of the angel. Or perhaps he mistakes the angel for the Lord. In any case, he is reproved for this (Acts 10:25–26). *the testimony about Jesus.* This phrase is used twice. It is possible to interpret it two ways. It may refer to those who have borne witness to Jesus. The angel is in this category. If this is the correct rendering, the second time it is used it would mean that the testimony to Jesus is the substance of all prophecy. This phrase can mean, however, the testimony Jesus bore to the churches and which they held. It is used this way three times previously in Revelation (1:2,9; 12:17). If this is the case, the second use of the phrase would mean that the message attested by Jesus is the essence of prophetic proclamation.

SESSION 8
The Rider on the White Horse
REVELATION 19:11–21

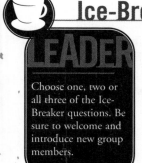

Last Week

Last week we listened to the greatest of all hallelujah choruses, as all creation gathered for the wedding feast of the Lamb. This week we will meet the Groom, who appears here as the great conquering warrior leading forth his hosts. This is none other than Jesus, the King of Kings and Lord of Lords.

Ice-Breaker   15 Min.

CONNECT WITH YOUR GROUP

LEADER

Choose one, two or all three of the Ice-Breaker questions. Be sure to welcome and introduce new group members.

Everyone enjoys "what if" questions once in a while: what if you had a million dollars, what if you ruled the world? Here are some more to consider. Take a few minutes to get to know one another with the following questions.

1. If you were a bird, what would you be?

- ○ Eagle.
- ○ Crow.
- ○ Sparrow.
- ○ Hummingbird.
- ○ Woodpecker.
- ○ Bluebird.
- ○ Other _____.

2. If you were a king or queen, what metal would be most prominent in your palace?

- ○ Gold.
- ○ Silver.
- ○ Stainless steel.
- ○ Pewter.
- ○ Cast iron.
- ○ Other _____.

3. What is the worst stain you've ever seen on someone's clothes?

Last week, we considered the church as the bride of Christ. This week we meet Jesus himself riding forth on a great white steed, leading his hosts to war. But the message is still the same: Jesus is the conquering hero, the faithful groom, who will not fail to achieve the purposes of God—the complete destruction of wickedness, and the eternal bliss of his faithful. Read the following passage from Revelation, then discuss the questions that follow.

The Rider on the White Horse

Reader One: [11]Then I saw heaven opened, and there was a white horse! Its rider is called Faithful and True, and in righteousness He judges and makes war. [12]His eyes were like a fiery flame, and on His head were many crowns. He had a name written that no one knows except Himself. [13]He wore a robe stained with blood, and His name is called the Word of God. [14]The armies that were in heaven followed Him on white horses, wearing pure white linen. [15]From His mouth came a sharp sword, so that with it He might strike the nations. He will shepherd them with an iron scepter. He will also trample the winepress of the fierce anger of God, the Almighty. [16]And on His robe and on His thigh He has a name written:

KING OF KINGS
AND LORD OF LORDS

Reader Two: [17]Then I saw an angel standing in the sun, and he cried out in a loud voice, saying to all the birds flying in mid-heaven, "Come, gather together for the great supper of God, [18]so that you may eat the flesh of kings, the flesh of commanders, the flesh of mighty men, the flesh of horses and of their riders, and the flesh of everyone, both free and slave, small and great."

[19]Then I saw the beast, the kings of the earth, and their armies gathered together to wage war against the rider on the horse and against His army. [20]But the beast was taken prisoner, and along with him the false prophet, who had performed signs on his authority, by which he deceived those who accepted the mark of the beast and those who worshiped his image. Both of them were thrown alive into the lake of fire that burns with sulfur. [21]The rest were killed with the sword that came from the mouth of the rider on the horse, and all the birds were filled with their flesh.

Revelation 19:11–21

QUESTIONS FOR INTERACTION

LEADER

Refer to the Summary and Study Notes at the end of this passage as needed. If 30 minutes is not enough time to answer all of the questions in this section, conclude the Bible Study by answering question 7.

1. Whose blood stains the robe of the King of Kings?

   ○ His own.
   ○ His enemies'.
   ○ Both.
   ○ Other _____.

2. Why is the King clothed in bloody garments, while his army is arrayed in pure white linen? Why is he the only one with a weapon?

3. Why does the King's sword come from his mouth instead of his hand?

4. Why is the King's scepter made of iron rather than gold?

5. How does the "great supper of God" compare with the "marriage feast of the Lamb" from last week's lesson (v. 9)?

6. Who will be the "guests" at this grisly "supper?" Who will not be there?

7. How can a person know here and now whether his or her name is written in the book of life?

GOING DEEPER:

If your group has time and/or wants a challenge, go on to this question.

8. Why does the King of Kings have a name "that no one knows except himself?"

♥ Caring Time   15 Min.

APPLY THE LESSON AND PRAY FOR ONE ANOTHER

LEADER

Have you started talking with your group about their mission—perhaps by sharing the dream of multiplying into two groups by the end of this study of Revelation?

Jesus is not just the Lamb, he is also the Lion, the conquering King of Kings and Lord of Lords. It is sometimes easy to forget his power and might, but we must never lose sight of the fact that one day only those whose names are written in his book will be among his blessed throng.

1. If you are uncertain whether your name is in the book of life, stop now and ask that Jesus write it there.

2. How will the power and authority of the King of Kings and Lord of Lords govern your life this week?

3. Who do you know whose name may not be in the book of life? Spend extra time praying for those people, and keep a list for continued prayer.

🌍 Next Week

This week we were reminded that Jesus' victory has been purchased by himself, and himself alone; his followers are granted eternal life by his grace. We also remembered that this victory and grace were purchased at a high price, the very blood of the one who redeems us. In the coming week, pray for the people on your list from question 3 above. Next week we will witness the final judgment, the last outpouring of God's wrath.

Notes on Revelation 19:11–21

SUMMARY: The long-awaited event happens at last: Christ returns to deal with the powers of evil, clad as a warrior on a white horse with the army of heaven behind him. This is an event often foretold in the Bible, especially the Old Testament (Isa. 13:4; 31:4; 63:1–6; Ezek. 38–39; Joel 3; Zech. 14:3; Matt. 13:41–42; 2 Thess. 1:7; 2:8). The second coming of Christ is a central theme in the New Testament, though it is more often thought of in terms of the salvation of the saints than the destruction of evil.

19:11 *Faithful and True.* See 3:14. In Hebrew thought the two ideas are very similar, since truth was thought of more as "reliability" than as "correspondence to reality." The coming of Christ demonstrates that God can be depended upon to keep his promises to deal with evil.

19:12 *many crowns.* In contrast to the seven crowns of the dragon (12:3) and the 10 crowns of the beast (13:1), Jesus has many crowns. He is the King of kings and the Lord of lords, as the angel already revealed (17:14). The image of king is one that is strongly associated with Jesus throughout the New Testament (Mark 10:48; Acts 2:36; 1 Cor. 15:24–25; Phil. 2:9–11). *a name written.* He has already been called by the name Faithful and True (v. 11) and he will be named the Word of God in verse 13. He has a third name as well that is secret, hidden from people. In the first century, a name was considered more than merely a way of distinguishing one person from another. Names were thought to express the essence of a person. Perhaps this name expresses the essential nature of Jesus' being, which is a mystery that cannot be grasped by finite minds.

19:13 *a robe stained with blood.* Some think that this is not his own blood, but the blood of battle. In this passage Jesus comes not as the redeemer who dies for sins, but as the warrior who conquers evil. This parallels the image in Isaiah 63:1–6 of the figure who has the blood of his enemies on his garments. Others feel that the robe is stained with his own blood, shed on the cross. It

is with the blood of Christ that Satan is destroyed, not by the sword. It is also possible that John has both meanings in mind here. *the Word of God.* This is who John has long known Jesus to be. John begins his Gospel: "In the beginning was the Word, and the Word was with God, and the Word was God" (John 1:1). He begins his first epistle in much the same way: "That which was from the beginning, which we have heard, which we have seen with our eyes, which we have looked at and our hands have touched—this we proclaim concerning the Word of life" (1 John 1:1). Jesus is the embodiment of God's ultimate word to the world.

19:14 *The armies that were in heaven.* This may be an army of angels or it could be an army of the redeemed as 17:14 suggests (Zech. 14:5; Mark 8:38; Luke 9:26; 1 Thess. 3:13; 2 Thess.1:7). In either case, the army does not engage in battle. That is left to Christ alone (v. 21). *white.* They are dressed in the garb of heaven.

19:15 Three symbols in this verse, all taken from the Old Testament, describe the actions of the warrior. First, the weapon which he uses in this battle issues from his mouth, an image which is drawn from Isaiah 11:4 (1:16; 2:12,16). His sword is his Word; the same Word which was the source of all creation (John 1:1–3; Heb. 1:2). Second, he rules with a rod of iron, an image taken from Psalm 2:9. Such a rod speaks not of governing but of destruction. Third, he treads the winepress, which is by now a familiar image in Revelation (14:19), drawn originally from Isaiah 63:3.

19:16 *KING OF KINGS AND LORD OF LORDS.* This is the fourth name that is given to Christ. This is the name by which he reveals himself to those with whom he does battle.

19:17–18 This gruesome supper contrasts sharply with the wedding banquet of 19:6–10 (Ezek. 39:17–20).

19:18 *the flesh of everyone.* That is, all who bear the mark of the beast, a number which includes all kinds of people.

SESSION 9
The Final Judgment
REVELATION 20:1–15

Last Week

Last week, we saw Christ riding forth in power and majesty on a white horse, conquering his foes and leading his followers. This week we will begin to enjoy the unopposed reign of the Lamb, and we will witness the final judgment of those who have rejected his sacrifice for sin.

Ice-Breaker   15 Min.

CONNECT WITH YOUR GROUP

LEADER

Welcome and introduce new group members. Choose one, two or all three Ice-Breaker questions, depending on your group's needs.

Time travel and changing history are, of course, impossible, yet it is often fun to speculate just the same. How would you change history? What would you do with a time machine? Take a few minutes to get to know one another with the following questions.

1. If you could bring back to life one figure from history, who would it be and why?

   ○ Abe Lincoln.
   ○ Shakespeare.
   ○ Albert Einstein.
   ○ Other _____.

2. If you could travel back in time what period would you visit?

3. Have you ever visited a place that had natural springs of hot water? What was it like?

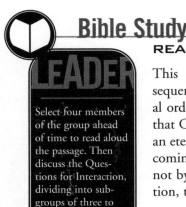

Bible Study

READ SCRIPTURE AND DISCUSS

Select four members of the group ahead of time to read aloud the passage. Then discuss the Questions for Interaction, dividing into subgroups of three to six.

This passage is difficult to put in any concrete chronological sequence, and has caused much debate over the years as to the actual order of final events. However, what we can be certain about is that Christ himself will throw Satan into the pit forever, setting up an eternal kingdom where he will rule unopposed. As we will see in coming lessons, this kingdom will be characterized by life and joy, not by death and sorrow. Read the following passage from Revelation, then discuss the questions that follow.

The Final Judgment

Reader One: 20 Then I saw an angel coming down from heaven with the key to the abyss and a great chain in his hand. ²He seized the dragon, that ancient serpent who is the Devil and Satan, and bound him for 1,000 years. ³He threw him into the abyss, closed it, and put a seal on it so that he would no longer deceive the nations until the 1,000 years were completed. After that, he must be released for a short time.

Reader Two: ⁴Then I saw thrones, and people seated on them who were given authority to judge. I also saw the souls of those who had been beheaded because of their testimony about Jesus and because of God's word, who had not worshiped the beast or his image, and who had not accepted the mark on their foreheads or their hands. They came to life and reigned with the Messiah for 1,000 years. ⁵The rest of the dead did not come to life until the 1,000 years were completed. This is the first resurrection. ⁶Blessed and holy is the one who shares in the first resurrection! The second death has no power over these, but they will be priests of God and the Messiah, and they will reign with Him for 1,000 years.

Reader Three: ⁷When the 1,000 years are completed, Satan will be released from his prison ⁸and will go out to deceive the nations at the four corners of the earth, Gog and Magog, to gather them for battle. Their number is like the sand of the sea. ⁹They came up over the surface of the earth and surrounded the encampment of the saints, the beloved city. Then fire came down from heaven and consumed them. ¹⁰The Devil who deceived them was thrown into the lake of fire and sulfur where the beast and the false prophet are, and they will be tormented day and night forever and ever.

Reader Four: ¹¹Then I saw a great white throne and One seated on it. Earth and heaven fled from His presence, and no place was found for them. ¹²I also saw the dead, the great and the small, standing before the throne, and books were opened. Another book was opened, which is the book of life, and the dead were judged according to their works by what was written in the books.

¹³Then the sea gave up its dead, and Death and Hades gave up their dead; all were judged according to their works. ¹⁴Death and Hades were thrown into the lake of fire. This is the second death, the lake of fire. ¹⁵And anyone not found written in the book of life was thrown into the lake of fire.

Revelation 20:1–15

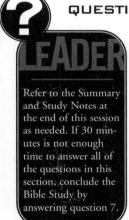

QUESTIONS FOR INTERACTION

Refer to the Summary and Study Notes at the end of this session as needed. If 30 minutes is not enough time to answer all of the questions in this section, conclude the Bible Study by answering question 7.

1. Note that there is no struggle when the angel "seized the dragon"—it almost seems effortless. What does this demonstrate about Satan's power in heaven?

2. We have, however, seen ample evidence in John's vision of Satan's power to "deceive the nations." What does this demonstrate about Satan's power here on earth?

3. What does Satan do the moment he is released from prison? What is the immediate response of mankind?

4. Who are thrown into the lake of fire? Why?

5. What is the "first resurrection?" Who will be brought to life at that time?

6. What is the "second death?" Who will be subject to it?

7. What disturbs you in this chapter? What gives you comfort?

GOING DEEPER:

If your group has time and/or wants a challenge, go on to this question.

8. Why does God release Satan one last time? What does it show about human nature that the world follows him again?

♥ Caring Time   15 Min.

LEADER

Have you identified someone in the group that could be a leader for a new small group when your group divides? How could you encourage and mentor that person?

The lake of fire is a place of eternal torment, created for Satan and his demons, but also to be occupied by those who choose to follow the evil one instead of Christ. The good news, however, is that the doors of heaven are open to all, and admission is free.

1. What aspect of heaven do you look forward to the most?

2. Pray for those who need salvation. In the coming week, seek an opportunity to share Christ's love with one of them.

3. Can you think of something that you can praise God for in your life?

Next Week

This week we learned about the 1,000-year reign of Christ, and watched as Satan was released one last time to deceive the nations away from God. In the coming week, pray for people you know who need to be rescued from the lake of fire, and ask God to give you an opportunity to share the Gospel with them. Next week we will begin a visit to the new Jerusalem, the eternal kingdom which God has prepared for us.

SUMMARY: The meaning of this passage has been the subject of great debate in the church. There are three main schools of thought when it comes to the Millennium (the thousand-year reign of Christ). Postmillennialists feel that the return of Christ will not occur until the kingdom of God has been established here on earth, in history as we know it. This will be the "golden age" of the church, a long reign of peace and prosperity. It will be followed by the Second Coming, the resurrection of the dead, the final judgment and the eternal kingdom. Amillennialists do not believe there will be a literal thousand-year reign of Christ. They see it as a metaphor for the history of the church between the resurrection of Christ and the Second Coming, during which those believers who have died will reign with Christ in heaven. When Christ returns there will be a general resurrection, the final judgment, and the start of Christ's reign over the new heaven and earth. They consider the binding of Satan to be what Christ did when he died on the cross (Matt. 12:29). Premillennialists believe that the events described in 20:1–6 will literally take place. Christ will return, the first resurrection will occur, and there will be a thousand years of peace in which Christ reigns here on earth. Then will come the final resurrection, the last judgment, and the new heaven and earth. The millennial reign is seen by some premillennialists as a special reward to the martyrs of chapter 6.

20:1 *Then I saw.* This phrase is used eight times in the section from the appearance of the rider on the white horse to the establishment of the new heaven and new earth (19:11, 17, 19; 20:1,4,11, 12; 21:1).

20:2 *bound him.* Somehow the power of Satan was curbed (Mark 3:27). *1,000 years* This could mean a long period of time during which the church spreads its influence around the world, or it could be a literal prediction of the order of final events.

20:4 This is an exceedingly difficult verse to analyze. *thrones.* It is impossible to know who is on these thrones beyond the fact that they will assist in the judging. Some suggest these are the apostles (Matt. 19:28), or all the saints (1 Cor. 6:2–3), or just those who overcame (3:21).

20:5 *The rest of the dead.* Most would say that this is the resurrection of unbelievers prior to the day of judgment.

20:6 *The second death.* The first death is the death of the body; the second death involves being cast into the lake of fire (v. 14; 21:8).

20:7–10 It has been suggested by some that the reason why Satan is released and allowed to gather another army is to show that God was right in his strong confrontation with evil. Even after a millennium of God's reign, Satan is able to gather an army of those who would oppose God and his rule. Man is totally without excuse. Even with the perfect government of the Lord Jesus, he is still discontented enough to be deceived by Satan.

20:8 *Gog and Magog.* In Ezekiel 38–39, there is an extended prophecy about "Gog, of the land of Magog." As in Revelation, the final battle follows the establishment of the messianic kingdom (Ezek. 36–37).

20:9 *the beloved city.* Jerusalem. *fire came down from heaven.* There is no battle this time. They are destroyed by the power of God (2 Kin. 1).

20:10 Satan joins the beast and the false prophet in the lake of fire. This is the final destination of evil in all its forms (Matt. 25:41). *the lake of fire and sulfur.* In the rest of the New Testament this is called *Gehenna* in Greek—translated "hell" in English (Matt. 5:22; Mark 9:43). The Valley of Hinnom, from which this name is drawn, was a place where human sacrifice took place (2 Kin. 16:3; 23:10; Jer. 7:31–32). It eventually became a kind of town dump where a fire perpetually smoldered, and thus it became a metaphor for hell.

20:12 *the book of life.* Another book is opened. In it are recorded the names of those who belong to Christ (3:5; 13:8; 21:27; Ex. 32:32–33; Dan. 12:1; Luke 10:20; Phil. 4:3). *according to their works.* The idea of judgment on the basis of one's works is found in the Old Testament and New Testament (Ps. 62:12; Jer. 17:10; Rom. 2:6; 1 Peter 1:17). The issue is not salvation by works but works as evidence of a person's relationship with God.

20:13 *Hades.* This is not the same as Gehenna. It is the place where departed souls go. It was thought of as an intermediate state (Luke 16:23; Acts 2:27).

20:15 Those who follow Satan experience the same fate as their master

SESSION 10
The New Jerusalem, Part 1
REVELATION 21:1–8

Last Week

In our last session, we witnessed God's final judgment upon the stubborn wickedness of mankind, and the final eternal destruction of Satan's power. This week we will find rest in the kingdom of God, as we get our first glimpse of the eternal home which he has prepared for us.

Ice-Breaker   15 Min.

CONNECT WITH YOUR GROUP

LEADER

Choose one or two of the Ice-Breaker questions. If you have a new group member you may want to do all three. Remember to stick closely to the three-part agenda and the time allowed for each segment.

Building a dream home may be your favorite daydream, or perhaps you'd be happy just to have a good remodeling of your present home. Either way, it's always fun to dream. Take a few minutes to get to know one another with the following questions.

1. Where would you place your ideal year-round dwelling?

    ○ By the sea.
    ○ By a lake.
    ○ In the mountains.
    ○ In the city.
    ○ By a stream.
    ○ Near a waterfall.
    ○ On a hill overlooking a great city.
    ○ In a gated community.
    ○ On a farm.
    ○ In a foreign country.
    ○ On an island.
    ○ In the woods.
    ○ Other _____.

2. If you could have one of the following made completely new, what would you choose?

- ○ My house.
- ○ My car.
- ○ My body.
- ○ My past.
- ○ My plans.
- ○ My relationships.
- ○ Other _____.

3. Have you ever been snorkeling or scuba diving? How deep did you go? What did you find that was interesting?

Bible Study   30 Min.
READ SCRIPTURE AND DISCUSS

Finally, after long battles against the enemy of mankind, we are brought into the eternal kingdom of God, the new Jerusalem. Now, for the first time in the history of our race, God will move his dwelling place from a distant heavenly throne and begin to live right along with man. Never again will we be prohibited from entering his presence, and for the first time since the fall of man we will be allowed to see his face! Read the following passage from Revelation, then discuss the questions that follow.

The New Jerusalem

John: **21** Then I saw a new heaven and a new earth, for the first heaven and the first earth had passed away, and the sea existed no longer. ²I also saw the Holy City, new Jerusalem, coming down out of heaven from God, prepared like a bride adorned for her husband. ³Then I heard a loud voice from the throne:

Voice: Look! God's dwelling is with men,
  And He will live with them.
  They will be His people,
  and God Himself will be with them and be their God.
  ⁴He will wipe away every tear from their eyes.

Death will exist no longer;
grief, crying, and pain will exist no longer,
because the previous things have passed away.

John: ⁵Then the One seated on the throne said,

God: "Look! I am making everything new."

John: He also said,

God: "Write, because these words are faithful and true."

John: ⁶And He said to me,

God: "It is done! I am the Alpha and the Omega, the Beginning and the End. I will give to the thirsty from the spring of living water as a gift. ⁷The victor will inherit these things, and I will be his God, and he will be My son. ⁸But the cowards, unbelievers, vile, murderers, sexually immoral, sorcerers, idolaters, and all liars—their share will be in the lake that burns with fire and sulfur, which is the second death."

Revelation 21:1–8

QUESTIONS FOR INTERACTION

Refer to the Summary and Study Notes at the end of this session as needed. If 30 minutes is not enough time to answer all of the questions in this section, conclude the Bible Study by answering question 8.

1. Why do you think God will create "a new heaven and a new earth?" How does this emphasize his complete victory over evil?

2. Why do you think that the sea will no longer exist?

3. What does it mean that the new Jerusalem will be "prepared like a bride adorned for her husband?" In practical terms, what would this mean for a city?

4. What is the significance of the names ascribed to God (v. 6), for those who are "victors" and those who are not? What do they mean to you, personally?

5. Where has God's dwelling been throughout human history? What is that dwelling like?

6. How will things be different when "God's dwelling is with men?" What will it be like when "God himself will be with them?"

7. What will life be like when "death will exist no longer?"

8. If God is going to "wipe away every tear" from our eyes, how should we view our sufferings and tears here and now? Does this promise help you to endure your tears "for a short time?"

GOING DEEPER:

If your group has time and/or wants a challenge, go on to this question.

9. Why does God say yet again, "It is done"? Why did Christ say "it is finished" on the cross? How are we to reconcile these many times when God has said this?

Caring Time _____ 15 Min.

APPLY THE LESSON AND PRAY FOR ONE ANOTHER

We are living on earth, where Satan is still active and powerful in deceiving many. But a glimpse of the kingdom that is to come should help encourage us to keep an eternal perspective, remembering that all we endure here is just preparing us to reign there.

1. Is your life characterized by any of the sins listed in verse 8? How will you purify yourself this week?

2. Is there any grief, crying or pain in your life right now? How can the group help you?

3. How can you prepare yourself to be "like a bride adorned for her husband?"

Next Week _____

This week we got our first glimpse of God's eternal kingdom, where he will at long last begin to dwell with mankind. He will personally wipe away every tear, and there will never again be any suffering, grief, or death. In the coming week, continue to pray for and reach out to those on your list of friends who need Christ, and pray also that the Lord will help you maintain a focus on his coming kingdom. Next week we will continue our tour of the new Jerusalem.

SUMMARY: The old order is done and finished. In its place there is a new order which John announces here. God himself announces that he will live among his people. The types of people who stand outside his kingdom are then listed.

21:1 *a new heaven and a new earth.* See Isaiah 11:6–9; 65:17; 2 Peter 3:13. *the first earth had passed away.* This event occurred in 20:11, described by means of a few terse sentences. *the sea existed no longer.* In ancient times the sea was often pictured as dark and mysterious; it was an enemy, not a friend. The lack of any seas in the new earth indicates how radically different the new will be.

21:2 *new Jerusalem.* The new Jerusalem will be described in detail in 21:9–22:5 (Gal. 4:26; Heb. 12:22). It was conceived of as the place where departed saints dwelt between the time of their death and the coming of the new heaven and the new earth (6:9–11; 2 Cor. 5:8; Phil. 1:23). It now descends to earth where it will finally rest. *prepared like a bride.* The church has already been pictured as the bride of Christ. John may intend the heavenly Jerusalem to be another metaphor for the church in the same way that Paul likens the church to the temple of God (1 Cor. 3:16; Eph. 2:21).

21:4 *He will wipe away every tear from their eyes.* The suffering is over; it is finished. No longer will there need to be a call to hold on and endure. *Death/grief/crying/pain.* All the old enemies of humanity are gone. Death itself is vanquished, so there will be no need anymore for mourning. Crying too is a thing of the past. Pain will be unknown.

21:5 *I am making everything new.* Creation, it seems, is not a static reality. Here at the end of history, God is still at work creating a new reality. That which was in principle true when an individual came to Christ—"If anyone is in Christ, he is a new creation" (2 Cor. 5:17)—is now consummated in fact. This process also includes the physical world (Rom. 8:21).

21:6 The voice from the throne (v. 3) is now identified. It is God who is speaking. This is an infrequent event in Revelation (1:8; 16:1,17). He speaks to assert that "It is done!" God's plan has been realized in its fullness. *the Alpha and the Omega.* The first and last letters in the Greek alphabet. God encompasses all of reality—all of what can be spoken and so is. *the Beginning and the End.* He also encompasses the whole of time. *I will give to the thirsty.* He satisfies the deepest needs—physical and spiritual—of humanity.

21:7 *The victor.* This recalls the letters to the seven churches and the promises made then (2:7,11,17,26; 3:5,12,21).

21:8 *cowards.* Those who do not stand up to the beast and his demands. *liars.* Those people who live in falsehood.

SESSION 11

The New Jerusalem, Part 2
REVELATION 21:9–21

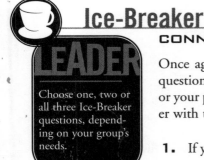

Last Week

In our last session we got our first glimpse of the eternal kingdom which God has prepared for us, in which there will be no death or suffering or tears. In this passage we will take a tour of that kingdom, and listen as John tries to describe the indescribable.

Ice-Breaker   15 Min.

CONNECT WITH YOUR GROUP

LEADER

Choose one, two or all three Ice-Breaker questions, depending on your group's needs.

Once again, let's spend a few minutes asking ourselves "what if" questions. Extend your imagination to design your perfect jewelry or your perfect home. Take a few minutes to get to know one another with the following questions.

1. If you could design a custom-made ring, what would you use?

- ○ Gold.
- ○ Silver.
- ○ Diamonds.
- ○ Pearls.
- ○ Emeralds.
- ○ Sapphires.
- ○ Other _____.

2. If you could build a dream house, what materials would you use?

- ○ Wood.
- ○ Brick.
- ○ Stone.
- ○ Cement.
- ○ Stucco.
- ○ Other _____.

3. What is the biggest city you've ever visited? Lived in?

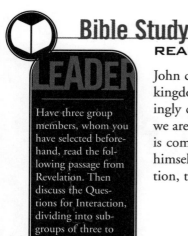

Bible Study   30 Min.

READ SCRIPTURE AND DISCUSS

John continues his description of the new Jerusalem, God's eternal kingdom that he has prepared for his saints. This passage is amazingly colorful and rich in detail, yet John is probably using things we are familiar with in hopes of partially describing something that is completely foreign to our experience: a kingdom in which God himself sits among men! Read the following passage from Revelation, then discuss the questions that follow.

The New Jerusalem

Reader One: [9]Then one of the seven angels, who had held the seven bowls filled with the seven last plagues, came and spoke with me:

Reader Two: "Come, I will show you the bride, the wife of the Lamb."

Reader One: [10]He then carried me away in the Spirit to a great and high mountain and showed me the holy city, Jerusalem, coming down out of heaven from God, [11]arrayed with God's glory. Her radiance was like a very precious stone, like a jasper stone, bright as crystal. [12]The city had a massive high wall, with 12 gates. Twelve angels were at the gates; on the gates, names were inscribed, the names of the 12 tribes of the sons of Israel. [13]There were three gates on the east, three gates on the north, three gates on the south, and three gates on the west. [14]The city wall had 12 foundations, and on them were the 12 names of the Lamb's 12 apostles.

Reader Three: [15]The one who spoke with me had a gold measuring rod to measure the city, its gates, and its wall. [16]The city is laid out in a square; its length and width are the same. He measured the city with the rod at 12,000 *stadia*. Its length, width, and height are equal. [17]Then he measured its wall, 144 cubits according to human measurement, which the angel used. [18]The building material of its wall was jasper, and the city was pure gold like clear glass.

Reader Two: [19]The foundations of the city wall were adorned with every kind of precious stone:
the first foundation jasper,
the second sapphire,
the third chalcedony,
the fourth emerald,
[20]the fifth sardonyx,

the sixth carnelian,

the seventh chrysolite,

the eighth beryl,

the ninth topaz,

the tenth chrysoprase,

the eleventh jacinth,

the twelfth amethyst.

Reader One: ^{21}The 12 gates are 12 pearls; each individual gate was made of a single pearl.

Reader Three: The broad street of the city was pure gold, like transparent glass.

Revelation 21:9–21

QUESTIONS FOR INTERACTION

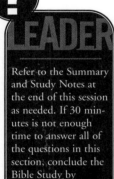

Refer to the Summary and Study Notes at the end of this session as needed. If 30 minutes is not enough time to answer all of the questions in this section, conclude the Bible Study by answering question 7.

1. Have you ever visited a church or cathedral that conveyed the grandeur and glory of God? What was it like?

2. What does the "massive high wall" around God's city suggest? Is it really necessary once all God's enemies are destroyed?

3. This wall has many gates. What does that suggest?

4. The city is approximately 1,500 miles square—roughly the distance from New York to Houston. What does this suggest?

5. Inside God's tabernacle of the Old Testament, the Holiest of Holies measured a perfect cube (1 Kin. 6:20), which is also true of this city (v. 16). What does this suggest about the new Jerusalem?

6. What is suggested by the opulence of the city with its pearls and gold and precious gems?

7. How do you feel about the fact that you will live forever in this city?

○ Excited.
○ Unworthy.
○ Bored.
○ Mystified.
○ Other _____.

GOING DEEPER:

If your group has time and/or wants a challenge, go to this question.

8. Why is there an angel at each gate?

♥ Caring Time   15 Min.

APPLY THE LESSON AND PRAY FOR ONE ANOTHER

LEADER

Conclude the prayer time by asking God for guidance in determining the future mission and outreach of this group.

A vision of God's new Jerusalem is both encouraging and sobering: encouraging because we are confident that all God's people will one day dwell there; sobering because we also know that some of the people in the world around us will not.

1. Are you a citizen of the new Jerusalem?

2. What aspect of God's city interests you the most?

3. Review the list of unsaved friends from last week. Has anyone reached out to these people in the past week?

Next Week

This week we got another glimpse of the eternal kingdom that is coming, the kingdom in which God will dwell with men. In the coming week, continue to pray for those on your list who need salvation, and ask God for an opportunity to share the Gospel with them. Next week we will learn more about the new Jerusalem, and will drink from the river of life and eat from the tree of life!

Notes on Revelation 21:9–21

SUMMARY: The fourth and final vision (1:10; 4:1; 17:3) is a detailed description of the New Jerusalem. In chapter 11:1 John was asked to measure the inner area of the temple. The idea there was of setting aside for preservation or for destruction. But here the city is measured to show its magnificence (Ezek. 40–41).

21:9 The language used here by the angel parallels that in 17:1, where John is shown the great harlot, Babylon. The contrast between the two cities is striking.

21:11 The New Jerusalem is characterized by the very radiance of God.

21:12 *Twelve angels were at the gates.* See Isaiah 62:6. *the names of the 12 tribes.* See Ezekiel 48:30–34.

21:14 *the 12 names of the Lamb's 12 apostles.* The very foundation of the city rests on the apostles of Jesus (Eph. 2:20). The church was, of course, the result of the labors of the Twelve following the death and resurrection of Jesus. With the names of the 12 tribes at the gates and the names of the 12 apostles at the foundation, it is clear that the New Jerusalem encompasses both Israel and the church. All of God's people have a place here.

21:16 *12,000 stadia.* It is an enormous city, beyond what any earthly city was or could be. Each of its four sides was approximately 1,500 miles long. By way of perspective, the distance from the Dead Sea to the Sea of Galilee is only 60 miles. Of course, the numbers may be symbolic. By them, John struggles to convey the vastness of the city. *Its length, width, and height are equal.* The New Jerusalem is a cube, as high as it is wide. The inner sanctuary of the temple was a perfect cube (1 Kings 6:20), a symbol of perfection.

21:17 *144 cubits.* It is not clear whether this was the thickness or the height of the walls. Of course, such a city would not need walls which, in ancient days, were a defense against enemies. This is God's city, and all his enemies have been destroyed. This illustrates again the fact that John is using metaphorical language. He is straining to describe that which defies description. The details of his description are not what is crucial; it is the total vision which he is seeking to express—which, in this case, is of a city so magnificent, so enormous, so secure that it can scarcely be imagined. This is the final dwelling place of God's people.

21:18 This city is built of materials unlike those used in any human city. *jasper.* A green, translucent crystal. This is the third time this mineral has been mentioned (v. 11; 4:3; see also v. 19). In verse 11, such jasper was said to glow with the very radiance of God. Thus the whole city would be aglow with God. The word jasper was used for various gemstones. The walls of the city are made of this precious stone. *pure gold like clear glass.* Gold has long been considered very precious, and here is a city of gold! This is unlike ordinary gold, however, since it is transparent.

21:19–20 John next describes the 12 foundations of the city, each of which is decorated with a different precious mineral. These are not ordinary foundations that are hidden under the earth. These are visible for all to see. On them are written the 12 names of the apostles (v. 14). These 12 minerals are similar to eight of the 12 gems in the breast piece of the high priest (Ex. 28:17–21). The stones mentioned here are difficult to identify, because their names do not always correspond to modern gems by that name.

21:19 *sapphire.* A deep blue, transparent gem. *chalcedony.* Green silicate of copper found near Chalcedony in Asia Minor. *emerald.* A green gemstone.

21:20 *sardonyx.* An agate made up of layers of a red mineral by the name of sard, and white onyx. *carnelian.* Blood red. *chysolite.* Yellow topaz or golden jasper. *beryl.* A sea-green mineral. *topaz.* A greenish-gold or yellow mineral. *chrysoprase.* A type of quartz which was apple-green. *jacinth.* A bluish-purple mineral. *amethyst.* Another variety of quartz; it was purple and transparent.

21:21 *12 gates.* The gates of ancient cities were an important part of their defense. They were built into the wall, often with a tower as part of their construction. *12 pearls.* Pearls were of great value in the ancient world (Matt. 13:45–46; 1 Tim. 2:9). The pearls from which these gates were built must have been enormous; again, quite beyond anything on this earth. *The broad street.* This, like the city itself (v. 18), is made of pure gold.

SESSION 12

The River of Life
REVELATION 21:22–22:5

Last Week

Last week, we took a tour of the new Jerusalem, marveling at its beauty and splendor. This week our tour will continue, and we will encounter marvels far greater than just precious gems: we will learn that God dwells now in the presence of men, and gives freely from the tree of life!

Ice-Breaker   15 Min.

CONNECT WITH YOUR GROUP

Choose one, two or all three of the Ice-Breaker questions, depending on your group's needs.

Rivers of life, trees with 12 different fruits, days that never end ... such marvels do not exist in our world. But understanding the marvels that do exist can help us understand what will one day come true. Take a few minutes to get to know one another with the following questions.

1. If you were a tree, what would you be?

○ Fruity fig.
○ Mighty oak.
○ Ever-green pine.
○ Weeping willow.
○ Other _____.

2. What great rivers have you seen? What river impressed you the most?

3. Have you ever stayed up all night? Why?

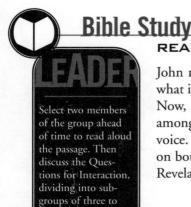

READ SCRIPTURE AND DISCUSS

LEADER

Select two members of the group ahead of time to read aloud the passage. Then discuss the Questions for Interaction, dividing into subgroups of three to six.

John now turns his attention from the construction of the city to what is contained in it, and this is where the real marvels are found. Now, for the first time since creation, God will make his home among men, and will allow us all to freely see his face and hear his voice. And, if that is not enough, he pours forth a river of life, lined on both sides with the tree of life! Read the following passage from Revelation, then discuss the questions that follow.

The River of Life

Reader One: [22]I did not see a sanctuary in it, because the Lord God the Almighty and the Lamb are its sanctuary. [23]The city does not need the sun or the moon to shine on it, because God's glory illuminates it, and its lamp is the Lamb. [24]The nations will walk in its light, and the kings of the earth will bring their glory into it.

Reader Two: [25]Each day its gates will never close because it will never be night there. [26]They will bring the glory and honor of the nations into it. [27]Nothing profane will ever enter it: no one who does what is vile or false, but only those written in the Lamb's book of life.

Reader One: 22 Then he showed me the river of living water, sparkling like crystal, flowing from the throne of God and of the Lamb [2]down the middle of the broad street of the city. On both sides of the river was the tree of life bearing 12 kinds of fruit, producing its fruit every month. The leaves of the tree are for healing the nations, [3]and there will no longer be any curse.

Reader Two: The throne of God and of the Lamb will be in the city, and His servants will serve Him. [4]They will see His face, and His name will be on their foreheads. [5]Night will no longer exist, and people will not need lamplight or sunlight, because the Lord God will give them light. And they will reign forever and ever.

Revelation 21:22–22:5

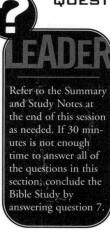

QUESTIONS FOR INTERACTION

Refer to the Summary and Study Notes at the end of this session as needed. If 30 minutes is not enough time to answer all of the questions in this section, conclude the Bible Study by answering question 7.

1. What does it mean that God and the Lamb are the sanctuary of the new Jerusalem? (Consider the various senses of "sanctuary," including "place of safety" and "site of sacrifices.")

2. In what way is the Lamb the "lamp" of God's glory?

3. Why do the gates of the city never close? What does this imply? What does this say to you about your relationship with God?

4. What might the "river of living water" symbolize?

5. Why would the river flow down the middle of the street? From the throne of God?

6. Read Genesis 3. What kind of tree is the tree of life described in Revelation? Why does it produce fruit all year? How do you see the whole of Scripture coming together in this book? How does it affect your trust in God?

7. What does it mean that "there will no longer be any curse?" How should this passage affect your life?

GOING DEEPER:

If your group has time and/or wants a challenge, go on to this question.

8. Read Exodus 33:18–23. What is the significance of God's people seeing his face?

Caring Time   15 Min.

APPLY THE LESSON AND PRAY FOR ONE ANOTHER

Following the Caring Time, discuss with your group how they would like to celebrate the last session next week. Also, discuss the possibility of splitting into two groups or continuing together with another study.

When God makes his dwelling among men, there will be no more weeping or pain or grief. To look upon God's face as a sinful being means instant death; but to look upon it in eternity will bring life and joy forever!

1. Are you longing to see God's face, or fearing it?

2. Do you feel that the gates to God's presence are open or closed? How can the group help?

3. What element of the "curse" seems most oppressive to you at present? How can the group pray for you?

Next Week

This week, we were permitted to see the river of life which flows right down the middle of the main street, freely available to all! In the coming week, continue to pray for those on your list whose names are not written in the book of life, and seek an opportunity to lead them to eternal life. Next week we will conclude this study with the joyful anticipation of Christ's imminent return.

Notes on Revelation 21:22–22:5

SUMMARY: John tells us of a scene that is filled with the radiant presence of God and the Lamb so brilliant that the New Jerusalem has no need of artificial illumination (Isa. 60:19–20; John 1:9; 8:12). In fact, it is never night (v. 25). Some speculate that this is a picture of universal salvation but it is more likely that John has simply adopted language from the prophets (as he has done throughout this section) in his attempt to convey the glory of the New Jerusalem. The focus now shifts from the city to the river of life that flows from the throne of God and of the Lamb.

21:22 *sanctuary.* The temple was the center of religious life in Israel. God was said to be present in the center of the temple, in the Holy of Holies. There is no need for a temple in the New Jerusalem because God is always present.

21:25 *its gates will never close.* The gates of a city were shut at night when there was the danger of a sneak attack (Isa. 60:11).

21:27 No one will have access to this utterly magnificent city unless his or her name is written in the Lamb's Book of Life.

22:1 The New Jerusalem is a place of eternal life. The saints will live eternally near this life-giving stream. *river of living water.* The idea of such a river is a common one in the Bible (Ps. 46:4; Ezek.

47:1–12; Zech. 14:8; John. 4:10–14). *from the throne.* God is the source of life.

22:2 *middle of the broad street.* The river of life is central to the New Jerusalem. *the tree of life.* The great story ends where it began, with the tree of life. In Genesis the tree of life in the Garden of Eden is lost to humanity by reason of sin (Gen. 2:9; 3:22). In Revelation it is restored. But what an awful price was paid for the sin in the intervening centuries. *12 kinds of fruit.* See Ezekiel 47:12.

22:3 *there will no longer be any curse.* What is left is God and the Lamb, reigning over all.

22:4 At long last too, men and women are able to behold the face of God. Gone are the intermediaries.

SESSION 13
Jesus is Coming Quickly!
REVELATION 22:6–21

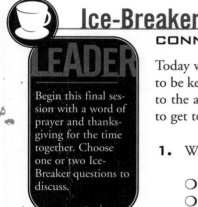

Last Week

Last week, we concluded our tour of the new Jerusalem, and learned that one day God will make his home right among mankind. This week, John will conclude his book with some final warnings and benedictions. One theme will come through in this last passage: God's will is completed quickly.

Ice-Breaker   15 Min.
CONNECT WITH YOUR GROUP

LEADER

Begin this final session with a word of prayer and thanksgiving for the time together. Choose one or two Ice-Breaker questions to discuss.

Today we will learn that God quenches all thirst, and that we need to be keeping our clothes clean in the meantime. It all comes down to the anticipation of seeing Jesus face to face. Take a few minutes to get to know one another with the following questions.

1. When you wash your clothes, do you:

   ○ Separate darks and lights?
   ○ Dump everything together?
   ○ Get someone else to do it?
   ○ Go to the cleaners?
   ○ Other _____?

2. When have you been the most painfully thirsty? How did you finally quench your thirst?

3. When you see Jesus face to face, what is the one question you'd like to ask him?

Bible Study

READ SCRIPTURE AND DISCUSS

LEADER

Select three members of the group ahead of time to read aloud the passage. Have one member read the part of John, another member read the part of the Angel, and the third read the part of Jesus. Then discuss the Questions for Interaction, dividing into subgroups of three to six.

In this final passage of the book of Revelation, John concludes with the reiterated theme that God carries out his plans quickly. This serves as both an encouragement and a warning: an encouragement to those suffering in persecution or sorrow; a warning for all that, when Christ returns, there will be no time for change. Read the following passage from Revelation, then discuss the questions that follow.

Jesus Is Coming!

John: ⁶Then he said to me,

Angel: "These words are faithful and true. And the Lord, the God of the spirits of the prophets, has sent His angel to show His servants what must quickly take place."

Jesus: ⁷"Look, I am coming quickly! Blessed is the one who keeps the prophetic words of this book."

John: ⁸I, John, am the one who heard and saw these things. When I heard and saw them, I fell down to worship at the feet of the angel who had shown them to me. ⁹But he said to me,

Angel: "Don't do that! I am a fellow slave with you, your brothers the prophets, and those who keep the words of this book. Worship God."

John: ¹⁰He also said to me,

Angel: "Don't seal the prophetic words of this book, because the time is near. ¹¹Let the unrighteous go on in unrighteousness; let the filthy go on being made filthy; let the righteous go on in righteousness; and let the holy go on being made holy."

Jesus: ¹²"Look! I am coming quickly, and My reward is with Me to repay each person according to what he has done. ¹³I am the Alpha and the Omega, the First and the Last, the Beginning and the End.

¹⁴"Blessed are those who wash their robes, so that they may have the right to the tree of life and may enter the city by the gates. ¹⁵Outside are the dogs, the sorcerers, the sexually immoral, the murderers, the idolaters, and everyone who loves and practices lying.

¹⁶"I, Jesus, have sent My angel to attest these things to you for the churches. I am the Root and the Offspring of David, the Bright Morning Star."

John: ¹⁷Both the Spirit and the bride say, "Come!" Anyone who hears should say, "Come!" And the one who is thirsty should come. Whoever desires should take the living water as a gift.

¹⁸I testify to everyone who hears the prophetic words of this book: If anyone adds to them, God will add to him the plagues that are written in this book. ¹⁹And if anyone takes away from the words of this prophetic book, God will take away his share of the tree of life and the holy city, written in this book.

²⁰He who testifies about these things says,

Jesus: "Yes, I am coming quickly."

John: Amen! Come, Lord Jesus!

²¹The grace of the Lord Jesus be with all the saints. Amen.

Revelation 22:6–21

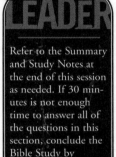

QUESTIONS FOR INTERACTION

Refer to the Summary and Study Notes at the end of this session as needed. If 30 minutes is not enough time to answer all of the questions in this section, conclude the Bible Study by answering question 7.

1. Note how often John uses the word "quickly" here. Does it seem, from earthly perspective, that God's plan is concluding quickly? How can this heavenly perspective help us in times of hardship?

2. For the second time, John falls into the error of worshiping an angel. What does this tell us of the temptation and danger of "worshiping" God's ministers and messengers?

3. What does it mean to wash one's robes (v. 14)? How are we to keep our robes clean?

4. "The Spirit and the bride say, 'Come!' Anyone who hears should say, 'Come!'" What does this mean to us as Christians today? How are we to come? How are we to *say* "come?"

5. John reiterates that "the time is near," then states that the unrighteous and the righteous should go on being what they are. What does this suggest about the sudden return of Christ? Will there be time for change on that day?

6. John closes his vision with a cry to God, urging Jesus to come again soon. Why would he desire this, given all the bad things we've witnessed in the vision?

7. How have you prepared yourself for Christ's return? Are you among the blessed who keep the words of this book?

GOING DEEPER:

If your group has time and/or wants a challenge, go on to this question.

8. John assures us (v. 8) that he, the "beloved apostle," personally "heard and saw these things" in the book of Revelation. How does this lend credibility to the truths we have been studying? Why should we as modern Christians take them very seriously?

APPLY THE LESSON AND PRAY FOR ONE ANOTHER

LEADER

Conclude this final Caring Time by praying for each group member and asking for God's blessing in any plans to start a new group or to continue studying together.

This is our last session in the book of Revelation, and we have been confronted with many truths. Most notable among those truths are the power of God which controls all events of human history; the reality of God's kingdom, available only to those whose names are written in the book of life; and the terrible reality of the lake of fire, where all those whose names are not written in the book of life will spend eternity. Remember to pray for those you know who may still be in need of God's salvation.

1. Are you like those who wash their robes, or more like those "outside" (vv. 14,15)?

2. How can the group be praying for you?

3. What do you think this group should do next?

  ○ Split into smaller groups.
  ○ Select another study.
  ○ Take time off.
  ○ Other _____.

Notes on Revelation 22:6–21

SUMMARY: Jesus affirms what he said at the beginning of the book (2:16; 3:11). In light of this fact, his people must always be alert, always prepared for his return. Once again Jesus repeats his reminder that he is returning soon (v. 7). The imminent return of Jesus is the context within which Revelation is to be read. Finally, a warning is affixed to the book. No one is to tamper with its contents, either to add to or take away from it (Deut. 4:2). This would be a real temptation with a book like this, whose message is mysterious, harsh at times, and often hard to understand. The temptation would be to leave out or explain away the parts that do not conform to one's views.

22:7 *coming quickly.* See 1 Corinthians 7:29–31 and 1 Thessalonians 4:15. *Blessed.* This is the sixth beatitude. *keeps the prophetic words of this book.* The important thing for believers is to realize that the aim of the book is not so much to inform the church about the details of the last days as it is to call the church to faithful living in the midst of the struggle it faces with evil in what-

ever historical context it finds itself. It sets this struggle in the larger context of the struggle between God and Satan and assures the church of the final outcome.

22:8 As he did at the beginning of the book (1:1, 4), here at the end John identifies himself. All that is necessary is a single name, John. The church knows who he is. *heard and saw these things.* This book is the record of visions John had. He did not create this out of his imagination; nor is it a literary creation derived from the Old Testament. He put down in words what was revealed to him. *I fell down to worship.* Once again (as in 19:10), John is so overwhelmed by what has been revealed to him that all he can do is worship.

22:10 *Don't seal the prophetic words of this book.* What has been revealed to John is for all people to read and heed. *the time is near.* Once again, he reiterates that the Second Coming is drawing near.

22:11 This verse must be read alongside verse 17. It is not that repentance is impossible as this verse might appear to say. There is an open invitation for all to come to the water of life ("whoever wishes"). But the fact is that with the end drawing close, people will persist in those behaviors that have come to express who they are and which identify to whom they belong.

22:13 Those words that were applied to God in 1:8 and 21:6 are now applied to Jesus. Jesus' right to judge is found in who he is.

22:14 *Blessed.* The final beatitude in the book of Revelation. *wash their robes.* An allusion to chapters 3:4 and 7:14. Those who are blessed are those who, by faith, have participated in the redeeming death of Jesus. *the right to the tree of life.* Those who are thus clad in the righteousness of Jesus have access to the very life of God (22:1–5). *enter*

the city by the gates. Furthermore, they have access to the city of God, the New Jerusalem where they will live eternally.

22:15 In contrast is the fate of those who have not been redeemed by the Messiah. The idea is not that there is a heavenly city which is surrounded by the enemies of God. Their fate has already been described (21:8). The point is the sharp contrast between the two outcomes as John prepares to invite all to come to that city (v. 17).

22:16 Jesus speaks again, attesting to the authenticity of this book. He reiterates what was said in 1:1—that this vision has come from Jesus to the angel to John to the churches. *Jesus.* The one who reveals all this is the man from Nazareth, who lived and taught and died on earth and then rose again. *the Root and the Offspring of David.* He is the messianic King from the line of David (5:5; Matt. 1:1; 9:27; 15:22; 21:9; Rom. 1:3). The image of a shoot that grows out of the stump of David is taken from Isaiah 11:1. *the Bright Morning Star.* See Numbers 24:17, which is understood to be a prophecy about the Messiah.

22:19 *his share of the tree of life.* The second part of the warning (about taking away) is addressed specifically to those who are believers.

22:20 For the third time in this epilogue, the reader is reminded that Jesus is coming soon. *Amen. Come, Lord Jesus!* John's response to this declaration is: "So be it; let it happen; Come Lord Jesus."

Personal Notes

_____

_____

_____

_____

_____

_____

_____

_____

_____

_____

_____

Personal Notes

Personal Notes

_____

_____

_____

_____

_____

_____

_____

_____

_____

_____

_____

_____

Personal Notes

_____

_____

_____

_____

_____

_____

_____

_____

_____

_____

Personal Notes

Personal Notes

_____

_____

_____

_____

_____

_____

_____

_____

_____

_____

_____

Personal Notes

_____

_____

_____

_____

_____

_____

_____

_____

_____

_____

_____

_____

Personal Notes

_____

_____

_____

_____

_____

_____

_____

_____

_____

_____

_____

Personal Notes

Personal Notes

_____

_____

_____

_____

_____

_____

_____

_____

_____

_____

_____

_____

Personal Notes